CREATING SUCCESS

Dealing with
Difficult People

Roy Lilley

**KOGAN
PAGE**

London and Philadelphia

For ATR, who deals with the most difficult person I know

First published 2002
Reprinted 2002 (twice), 2003, 2004 (twice), 2005
Reissued in 2006
Reprinted 2006, 2007, 2008

Kogan Page Limited
120 Pentonville Road
London N1 9JN
United Kingdom
www.koganpage.com

Kogan Page US
525 South Street, #241
Philadelphia PA 19147
USA

© Roy Lilley 2002, 2006

ISBN-10 0 7494 4751 6
ISBN-13 978 0 7494 4751 9

British Library Cataloguing in Publication Data

A CIP record for this book is available from the British Library

Library of Congress Cataloging-in-Publication Data

Lilley, Roy C.
    Dealing with difficult people / Roy Lilley.
        p. cm. -- (Creating success)
    Reprint. Originally published in 2002.
    Includes bibliographical references.
    ISBN 0-7494-4751-6
    1. Psychology, Industrial. 2. Interpersonal conflict. 3. Problem employees. I. Title. II. Series.
HF5548.8.L493 2006
650.1'3--dc22
                                        2006014888

Typeset by Jean Cussons Typesetting, Diss, Norfolk
Printed and bound in India by Replika Press Pvt Ltd

Contents

About this book

This is not a book to be read from cover to cover. It is not *War and Peace*, although with a bit of luck it will give you some ideas on how to have more peace than war.

It is a book to dip into, look for the character or situation you're having problems with, find a solution, apply it and move on. Life is too short to spend it having a row with people.

This is a book to scribble on the pages, rip bits out and do all the things with that your old school would give you detention for! This is a source book but not a reference book. A book to dive into but not to get immersed in.

This is a book you can use to improve your own performance or use as a source of ideas to work in groups to improve the performance of your team.

If all else fails it is a book just heavy enough to throw at someone who is being really difficult, without the risk of doing them any serious damage!

To the uninitiated, difficult people can be the bane of your life, a blot on your landscape and a real pain to work with. This book is designed to help you to enjoy difficult people. Once you have the key, you can unlock them, influence them, get them working for you and they'll never notice.

What else will you find...?

 Think about it!

The light bulb will prompt you to think about an idea, spare a thought for a new approach or to take on board something different

 Hazard warning

The hazard warnings point out traps and problems for the unwary. They say, 'Beware, get this right, or you're in trouble!'

These are good ideas, short cuts and ways to cut through the dross and the jungle.

The coffee cup says, it's time to read something thoroughly, so make yourself comfortable. Or it says enough is enough, take a break!

dealing with difficult people

The first rule:

There is no such thing as a difficult person, there are just people we need to learn how to deal with...

The second rule:

Re-read the first rule...

A short course in human relations

This book is all about dealing with difficult people. Get it? Not difficult situations or difficult issues. It's the people we are focusing on. Certainly difficult people will give you a bad time, horrible situations and awkward issues to overcome. However, at the centre of it all are the people. By understanding people, how they tick, what they think and why they act like they do, we can avoid the bad times and horrible situations, and overcome the awkward issues.

The six most important words: *'I admit, I made a mistake.'*
The five most important words: *'You did a good job.'*
The four most important words: *'What is your opinion?'*
The three most important words: *'Would you mind?'*
The two most important words: *'Thank you.'*
The one most important word: *'We.'*

The least important word: *'I.'*

If we plant some seeds and the flowers don't bloom – it's no good blaming the flower. It may be the soil, the fertiliser, not enough water? Who knows? We just find out what the problem is and fix it.

If we have difficulties with our families, the people we work with or our friends, what's the point of blaming them? Figure out the reason and then fix it.

Difficult, who me?

Yes, you! Before you can think about dealing with difficult people, let's start with you. Are you difficult? Are you the one out of step? Are you the one with the problem?

Here's some bad news for you: nice people are not always like you! Yes, yes, I know the world would be a much simpler place if everyone was like you, but they're not. They will have different backgrounds, different education, different perspectives and different ambitions. They will be motivated differently and think differently. And they can still be nice people!

Really difficult people are most likely to be selfish and inwardly focused. They won't give a toss about you. For them, it's all about them. So, don't let them get under your skin.

So the number one rule in dealing with difficult people is:

Don't take it personally!

OK, so what do you do? Easy. Ask yourself this question:

What do I want to get out of this encounter?

Decide, in advance:

- what is the purpose of the encounter;
- what are the key results you want to achieve;
- whether you need to change your behaviour to get the most out of the encounter.

This doesn't mean you have to let a rude pig trample all over you. But it does mean you don't get into a bare knuckle fight.

✓ TIP

Someone been rude to you? Try this: 'I'm not sure quite what you meant by that remark. Can you explain it to me please?' It usually means they will tone down. As they calm down, don't forget the 'please'!

Think about it! The brutal truth is they don't care about you.

This may come as something of a shock, but there aren't too many people out there who care too much about you. There's your mother, she probably still loves you; family, partners and a few friends, maybe. But, when push comes to shove, you're on your own.

How we treat each other is largely a product of how we feel about each other. Most folk start off neutral, some downright antagonistic, but the fact is most people couldn't care less about you.

It gets worse! Difficult people don't care about you at all.

They care about themselves. They are into them, in a big way. That's why they're difficult.

What can you do about it? The brutal answer is not much! It is very unlikely that you will change them. Why bother? There is a much easier way.

Remember this: *Difficult people are predictable people.*

✓ TIP

Avoid having a row. If you can, don't argue. Settle a dispute by looking for a higher authority that is neutral. A rule book, systems protocol, service manual or company policy may provide the answer. Don't get personal.

That simple fact makes your life much easier. How many times have you heard folk say 'Oh, don't bother with him, he's a misery.' Or 'Don't ask her, she finds fault in everything.'

You see, difficult people are not just difficult with you. They are into themselves and are, usually, difficult with everyone. Predictable is easy. You can prepare for difficult people, you can plan for them, you can plot, scheme and collude against them. They are stuck in their ways. All you have to do is manoeuvre.

This doesn't mean becoming a soft touch, or a pushover. It means you use your brains more than your emotions. The trick is to decide in advance what you want out of an encounter, plan accordingly and go for it.

If you know someone is a nit-picker and a stickler for detail – give them detail. *'In the report I've included all the background I can think of, including spreadsheets for four scenarios. Let me know if there's something else you need.'*

If someone is abrupt, get straight to the point, avoid flannel and go to the heart of the matter. *'I know you are very busy, so I'll come straight to the point. What do you think about this next phase of the development?'*

If someone is an egomaniac, tell them how good they are. *'Jane, I know you are the neighbourhood expert on this, so I've put the detail together and made a couple of recommendations. But can I leave it to you to come up with some alternative directions, if you think they might be better?'*

The strategy is easy. You won't change a difficult person by being difficult. They don't care about you, they care about themselves. By deciding what you want out of the encounter and being prepared to manoeuvre, trim, sidestep, change, call it what you like, you end up winning. You end up getting what you want.

It's so easy that you will end up wishing everyone was difficult – because the difficult ones are easiest to manage!

A quick guide to the seven classically difficult types

– or how to sound like an expert in the time it takes to drink a cup of coffee

> Too busy to read the whole book right now? That's fine, take a break and read these next few pages – it's all you need for now. You'll be an expert!

Recognise anyone?

There are seven basic personality types that get filed in the difficult tray. Elsewhere in this book I deal with many more types, but they are derivatives of the seven deadly sinners. Here's the quick guide to becoming an expert.

Hostile, aggressive, belligerent and offensive

Charming types: I thought I'd get these out of the way right from the start. These charmers can be frightening, alarming and downright terrifying. They are often bullies and control freaks.

A management guru called Bramson, back in 1988, made the whole thing more complicated by identifying three types of aggressive people:

■ the Sherman tank;
■ the sniper;
■ the exploder.

They are all horrible, in their own way. And each has to be dealt with using a slightly different approach. The tank, sniper and exploder are such good metaphors that they almost explain themselves.

Here's Bramson's advice about the Sherman tank:

> The term Sherman Tank accurately depicts what a hostile person does. They come out charging. They are abusive, abrupt, intimidating, and overwhelming. They attack individual behaviours and personal characteristics. They bombard you with unrelenting criticisms and arguments. Sherman Tanks usually achieve their short-run objectives, but at the cost of lost friendships, and long-term erosions of relationships.
>
> Sherman Tanks have a strong need to prove to themselves and others that their view of the world is right. They have a strong sense of how others should act, and they are not afraid to tell them about it.
>
> Sherman Tanks value aggressiveness and confidence. This belief causes them to devalue individuals they perceive as not having those qualities.
>
> The basic core belief of a Sherman Tank is, 'If I can make you out to be weak, faltering, or equivocal, then I will seem, to myself and others, strong and sure.'

Now the sniper. Snipers are not in the least bit like the Sherman tank but they are just as deadly. Back to Bramson:

Snipers prefer a more covered approach. They put up a front of friendliness behind which they attack with pot shots, use innuendoes, nonplayful teasing and not so subtle digs. Snipers use social constraints to create a protected place from which to strike out at objects of anger or envy.

They pair their verbal missiles with non-verbal signals of playfulness and friendship. This creates a situation where any retaliation back at the Sniper can be seen as an aggressive act, like you are doing the attacking not the defending.

Much like the Sherman Tank, Snipers believe that making others look bad makes them look good. They also have a strong sense of what others should be doing, but their constant cutting remarks usually demotivates colleagues rather than producing results.

Finally, the exploder. Exploders are characterised by fits of rage-fuelling attacks which seem barely under control. Bramson says:

These tantrums can erupt out of conversations and discussions that seem to start friendly. Usually these tantrums occur when the exploder feels physically or psychologically threatened. In most cases an Exploder's response to a threatening remark is first anger followed by either blaming or suspicion.

Complainer, grouches and the sourpuss

Complainers moan like hell about everything but never seem to take any action to change anything. It is almost as if they like having something to moan about.

Complainers are not the individuals who have legitimate complaints and a desire to find a solution to the problem. The complainer is someone who finds fault in everything. Sometimes they do have a real complaint, but rarely do they want to find a way to fix the problem.

Here's what the guru Bramson said about them:

The constant complaints can cause people around the complainer to feel defensive.

Complainers view themselves as powerless, prescriptive, and perfect. These beliefs cause complainers to convert useful problem solving into complaining. Their feeling of powerlessness causes them to think that they cannot change things so they had better complain to people who can.

Their prescriptive attitude gives them a strong sense for how things ought to be and any deviation from that produces complaints. Complaints are a way for the complainer to confirm that they are not in control or responsible for things that are done wrong, reaffirming perfectionism.

 Let's think about this

Given that moaners and groaners have a strong sense of how things should be, could you harness their energy to enable them to change things to how they ought to be? It is important to take on board the idea that just because someone has certain character traits they are not necessarily a write-off. Dealing with difficult people is about just that – dealing with them and using the talents they do have. Good management is about getting the best out of everyone.

The silent unresponsive and the quiet ones

A silent, unresponsive person deals with any disagreeable situation by shutting down. Ask them what they think and you'll be rewarded with a grunt! (Bit like a teenage son!)

Let's turn to the work of another management psychologist and organisation dynamics guru. Lewis-Ford wrote in 1993:

The unresponsive use silence as their defensive weapon, to avoid revealing themselves, so they can avoid reprimand. (Just like a teenage son!) On the other hand it can be used as an aggressive, offensive device as a way to hurt you by denying access. An unresponsive person in some cases might be distrusting of others, which explains their need to clam up.

Sometimes, keeping the silence is used as a way to avoid one's own reality. When words are spoken, they reveal thoughts or fears of the thinker, which can be frightening. It can be used to mask fear, sullen anger, or it can be a spiteful refusal to co-operate.

This type of person can be maddeningly difficult to deal with because of the communication barrier they put up. *(Very like a teenage son!)* In most cases, this person will not be very willing to converse openly. When they speak, there might be prolonged periods of silence due to a lack of confidence in themselves and their lives. This can result in a breakdown of communication, which leads to an unproductive interaction.

Those who portray this type of behaviour usually display such body language as staring, glaring, frowning, or folded arms in an uncomfortable position.

 Let's think about this

OK, so the joke is on the teenage son. Perhaps there are a few teenage daughters who fit the description, too! Think about Lewis-Ford's writing, *'The unresponsive use silence as their defensive weapon, to avoid revealing themselves, so they can avoid reprimand.'* Time to have a family chat – perhaps!

The super agreeable: a bit like a spaniel puppy

The super agreeable is always reasonable, sincere, and supportive to your face but doesn't always deliver as a promised – with apologies to spaniel owners everywhere!

They want to be friends with everyone, love the attention. However, there's a darker side. They tend to lead you on with deceptive hints and references to problems that have been raised, and will willingly agree to your plans of accomplishing the task at hand, only to let you down by not delivering.

Back to Bramson for an astute description written over 13 years ago:

> Everyone needs to feel acceptance and to be liked by others. There is a balance point that integrates our needs to do a job well and to find a reasonable place in the pecking order with a reasonable concern for being liked.
>
> For this type of person, the burden is so far to one extreme that they feel an almost desperate need to be liked by everybody. Their method of gaining acceptance is to tell you things that are satisfying to hear. They also use humour as a way to ease their conversations with others.
>
> This type of difficult person presents a problem when they lead you to think that they are in agreement with your plans only to let you down. Their strong need to give and receive friendship can conflict with the negative aspects of reality.
>
> Rather than directly losing friendships or approval, they will commit themselves to actions on which they cannot or will not follow through.

 Let's think about this

Relationships, alliances, the workplace cannot function without them. A good manager recognises staff who take on more than they can deliver. To deny them a piece of work is, in their eyes, to deny them friendship. To snub them. There is a fine balance to be considered. Feelings can be easily damaged. Reality is often the very cold antidote to the warmth of friendship.

The negativist

The negative person is a corrosive influence on groups and can be very demotivating for the individual. Here's another expert, the psychologist Rosner. Someone else for you to quote and sound like an expert!

> The Negativist is best described as a personality that not only disagrees with any cumulative suggestions in a group situation, but also is the first

to criticise group progress. While their criticism could be interpreted as constructive, this disrupts progress in a work environment and could negatively impact interpersonal relationships within a working situation.

Another common reference to the negativist is the sceptic. Like the negativist these individuals like to tear apart and shoot holes in whatever is being said at the moment. They wear out their welcome over time as people catch on to their chronic negativity.

Inside the character of a person who is considered to be negative is a person who is having difficulties dealing with a deep seated inner conflict. This usually comes from a feeling that they don't have power over their own lives. The negativist is unable to work through basic human disappointment. A negativist believes that everyone can relate and understand the well of disappoint they feel towards humanity and our own imperfection.

While these people are so incredibly embittered about life and how it treats them, they are capable of having deep personal convictions at any task that is placed in front of them. However, if they are not in direct control of the project, it will fail because they believe that no one can handle or perform a task quite like they can.

 Let's think about this

Buried in all this negativity is the capacity for a 'deep personal conviction' and the ability to see through tasks where they have direct control. Everyone has something to offer. Can you live with the thought that there are no bad staff, just poorly performing managers?

The know-all

Know-alls have an overwhelming need to be recognised for their intellectual ability. They are bores, dull and very tedious!

Here are the thoughts of two eminent experts in the field of human behaviour. First Raffenstein:

Know-alls can provoke feelings of anger, resentment, sometimes even violence in others.

So watch out! The second expert, Keyton, took a less alarming approach when writing in 1999:

> The Know-all could be suffering from lack of self-importance or maybe unable to participate at the level in which he/she would like to contribute to the group's idea pool. Taking the time to listen to a Know-all's endless speeches could lead to loss of time in completing projects or assignments.

Know-alls are very complex people. They can be bullies. They appear so certain they are right, it seems pointless to argue. They can be very persuasive. They like to communicate as if they are talking to a child. Very annoying!

The second know-all type dominates conversations and likes being the centre of attention. The problem is if they read press cuttings on a subject, they are an expert. Some know-alls are not above making up for any information or knowledge deficit by inventing a few facts.

Our friend Bramson wrote:

> Know-alls' problems stem from a need for others to think of them as being important and respected. Usually people who are confronted with a situation involving a Know-all are faced with a frustration. This usually leads to tension in work relationships.

 Let's think about this

Is there a role for a know-all? If they like the power of knowledge, maybe the answer it to make them an expert. Send them on a course.

The indecisive, the ditherer, the hesitant

Inside the indecisive is a perfectionist trying to get out. They just can't seem to manage it. According to Bramson, this type of personality usually comes in two types. One wants things done his/her way or no way; the second is someone who, at times, intentionally drags out discussions by injecting different viewpoints, frustrating everyone in the process.

The indecisive person may be one who usually is not good at communicating their own thoughts, needs, and opinions to those around them. At best these people stall because they are unable to cope with stress at a high and low level.

In order to deal with the stress they procrastinate which brings down co-workers and other people around them. At best they stall by not considering alternative ways of getting a job done. So those on the receiving end of the indecision lose enthusiasm and commitment to the project or person which eventually brings down the team.

Despite their success in evading the decision, the typical indecisive gets stressed over a various amount of tension. This doesn't mean that they don't communicate a decision or feeling through indirect communications. In fact, they are masters in body language, low moans or grunts, or even eye contact.

If the indecisive chooses to verbally make contact with other people it comes out in short phrases or sentences. Many times, these pieces of information get either ignored or shoved aside by co-workers who are already frustrated by the lack of communication they have received from that person.

They are also sensitive and might withhold information because they are worried about how it will be perceived by a group or person they are communicating it to. If the information is not sensitive they feel that their opinions don't matter and that someone else will deal with a conflict or problem that they are worried about.

 Let's think about this

There's a challenge for you! Find them a role that doesn't involve communication or stress. Your call!

That's the end of the of the quick guide to the types of difficult people you will come across. Now you're an expert. Make another coffee and let's put that new found knowledge to work.

Calling on the experts gives us the fast-track to dealing with difficult people.

First the diagnosis

What type are they? Brad McRae, author of *Negotiations and Influencing Skills: The art of creating and claiming value*, suggests four steps to accurately diagnose someone:

■ The first thing to do is to watch and take notice if you've seen this behaviour in three other situations with this person. The reason for this is because the first two times are probably chance but by the third time it's probably a pattern.

■ The second thing to do is notice whether or not this person is dealing with a lot of stress. Stress may be causing this adverse behaviour and is not a regular occurrence.

■ The third thing to do is to ask yourself if you've been suffering from any exceptional stress. Stress on you may be causing you to see the world in a way that is contrary to what is actually going on.

■ The fourth: have you had an adult-to-adult conversation with this person? There are times when the other person may or may not know that his/her behaviour is causing a problem for you and talking to him or her can clear up what turns out to be a simple misunderstanding.

McRae tells us 'The reason people get into difficult situations with difficult people is because they allow themselves to become emotionally hooked. Often, the more we try to break free of these situations the more ensnared we become until some of us crack.'

Why do we get hooked, or sucked in to difficult people? Back to McRae: all people have a set of values or beliefs that guides their behaviour throughout life and especially in encounters with other people. Each individual's set of values is unique to him or her.

Here is McRae's list of fifteen of the most common core beliefs:

- I must be loved or accepted by everyone.
- I must be perfect in all I do.
- All the people with whom I work or live must be perfect.
- I can have little control over what happens to me.
- It is easier to avoid facing difficulties and responsibilities than to deal with them.
- Disagreement and conflict should be avoided at all costs.
- People, including me, do not change.
- Some people are always good; others always bad.
- The world should be perfect, and it is terrible and catastrophic when it is not.
- People are fragile and need to be protected from *the truth*.
- Others exist to make me happy, and I cannot be happy unless others make me happy.
- Crises are invariably destructive, and no good can come from them.
- Somewhere there is the perfect job, the perfect solution, the perfect partner and so on, and all I need to do is search for them.
- I should not have problems. If I do, it indicates I am incompetent.

■ There is one and only one way of seeing any situation the *true* way.

🍵 Time for another break. Take a quiet reflective moment. You won't understand others if you don't understand yourself. Which of McRae's values do you share?

If you can, take a look at yourself and decide which core value is, or was, hooked in a particular difficult situation you've had to deal with. Now you will understand why you were upset. The new understanding leads to controlling yourself and your emotions better.

According to McRae, if we learn the first step, to control ourselves, then we have a better chance to control others and the situations we find ourselves in.

Robert Bramson, author of *Coping With Difficult People*, lists tips for each of the seven types we will come across. Here is his 'at a glance guide'.

the type	the response
the hostile Sherman tank	■ Give them a little time to run down. ■ Don't worry about being polite; get in any way you can. ■ Get their attention, perhaps by calling them by name or sitting or standing deliberately. ■ Getting them to sit down is a good idea. ■ Maintain eye contact. ■ State your own opinions forcefully. ■ Don't argue with what the other person is saying or try to cut them down. ■ Be ready to be friendly.

the hostile sniper	■ Smoke them out. Don't let social convention stop you.
	■ Provide them with an alternative to a direct contest.
	■ Don't focus on their point of view, be sure to involve everybody.
	■ Do move fast to try to solve any problems that arise.
	■ Prevent sniping by setting up regular problem-solving meetings.
	■ If you are a witness to a situation with a Sniper, stay out of it, but insist that it stop in front of you.
the hostile exploder	■ Give them time to run down on their own.
	■ If they don't run down, cut into the tantrum with a neutral phrase such as 'Stop!'.
	■ Show them that you take them seriously.
	■ If possible, take a breather with them to the side and in private.
the complainer	■ Listen attentively to their complaints even if you feel guilty or impatient.
	■ Acknowledge what they are saying by paraphrasing their statements and checking out how you feel about it.
	■ Don't agree or apologise for their allegation even if, at the moment, you don't accept it as true.
	■ Avoid the accusation–defence– re-accusation ping-pong argument.
	■ State and acknowledge facts without comment.
	■ Try to move to a problem-solving mode by asking specific, information questions, assigning limited fact-finding tasks, or

	asking for the complaints in writing, but be serious and supportive about it. ■ If all else fails, ask the complainer, 'How do you want this discussion to end?'
the silent and the unresponsive	■ Rather than trying to interpret what the silence means, get them to open up. ■ Ask open-ended questions. ■ Wait as calmly as you can for a response. ■ Use counselling questions to help move them along. ■ Do not fill in the silence with your conversation. ■ Plan enough time to allow you to wait with composure. ■ Get agreement on or state clearly how much time is set aside for your 'conversation'. ■ If you get no response, comment on what's happening. End you comment with an open-ended question. ■ Again, wait as long as you can, then comment on what's happening and wait again. Try to keep control of the interaction by dealing matter-of-factly with 'Can I go now?' and 'I don't know' responses. ■ When they finally open up, be attentive and watch your impulse to gush. Flow with tangential comments. They may lead you to something relevant and important. If they don't, state your own need to return to the original topic. ■ If they stay closed, avoid a polite ending, terminate the meeting yourself and set up another appointment. At length, inform them what you intend to do, since a discussion has not occurred.

the super agreeable	■ You must work hard to surface the underlying facts and issues that prevent the super agreeable from taking action. ■ Let them know that you value them as people by telling them directly, asking or remarking about family, hobbies, wearing apparel. Do this only if you mean it, at least a little! ■ Ask them to tell you those things that might interfere with your good relationship. ■ Ask them to talk about any aspect of your product, service or self that is not as good as the best. ■ Be ready to compromise and negotiate if open conflict is in the wind. ■ Listen to their humour. There may be hidden messages in those quips or teasing remarks.
the negativist	■ Be alert to the potential, in yourself and in others in your group, for being dragged down into despair. ■ Make optimistic but realistic statements about past successes in solving similar problems. ■ Don't try to argue them out of their pessimism. ■ Do not offer solution-alternatives yourself until the problem has been thoroughly discussed and you know what you are dealing with. ■ When an alternative is being seriously considered, quickly raise the question yourself of negative events that might occur if the alternative were implemented. ■ At length, be ready to take action on your own. Announce your plans to do this without equivocation.

	■ Beware of eliciting negativist's responses from highly analytical people by asking them to act before they feel ready.
the know-all	■ Make sure you have done a thorough job of preparing yourself; carefully review all pertinent materials and check them for accuracy. ■ Listen carefully and paraphrase back the main points of the proposals, thus avoiding over-explanation. ■ Avoid dogmatic statements. ■ To disagree be tentative, yet don't equivocate; use the questioning form to raise problems. ■ Ask extensional questions to assist in the re-examination of plans. ■ As a last resort, choose to subordinate yourself to avoid static and perhaps to build a relationship of equality in the future. Where the know-all is not threatening or bullying: ■ State correct facts or alternative opinions as descriptively as possible and as your own perceptions of reality. ■ Provide a means for them to save face. ■ Be ready to fill a conversation gap yourself. ■ If possible, cope with them when they are alone.
the indecisive	■ Make it easy for the indecisive to tell you about conflicts or reservations that prevent the decision. ■ Listen for indirect words, hesitations and omissions that may provide clues to problem areas.

- When you have surfaced the issue, help them solve their problem with a decision.
- At times, their reservations will be about you. If so, acknowledge any past problems and state relevant data non-defensively, propose a plan and ask for help.
- If you are not part of the problem, concentrate on helping the indecisive examine the facts. Use the facts to place alternative solutions in priority order. This makes it easier if they have to turn someone else down.
- If real, emphasise the quality and service aspects of your proposal.
- Give support after the decision seems to have been made.
- If possible, keep the action steps in hands.
- Watch for signs of abrupt anger or withdrawal from the conversation. If you see them try to remove them from the decision situation.

3

A fast-track guide to conflict and how to handle it

What conflict is

The precise definition of 'conflict' is: a direct disagreement of ideas or interests, a battle or struggle, antagonism or opposition. Add to that incompatibility and interference and you get a pretty ugly picture.

However it is defined, you'll know it when you've got it. What's involved: or in guru speak, what are the dynamics of conflict?

There are two fundamentals at work:

■ the objective differences between the participants;
■ the emotions and perceptions that come as the gift wrapping.

People react to conflict in five basic ways: two 'P's and three 'C's:

1. Put it off. They will avoid it, pretend it doesn't exist and put off having to deal with it.
2. Put up with it: generally resulting in letting someone get his or her own way.
3. Compromise: they'll look for a win-win where both (or all sides) give up something to reach an agreed conclusion.
4. Carry on fighting: when one, both or all sides are not prepared to give ground and they carry on slugging it out until they drop!
5. Collaborate: when a mutually agreed solution is arrived at and every one has their needs addressed. Not necessarily met – but addressed.

Number 5, collaborating, is ideal – but it is the hardest to achieve. It needs two more 'P's, patience and persistence – with a few gallons of perspiration!

✓ TIP

It is important to recognise both of the elements of conflict. You can't deal with the differences in a clinical way without taking into account the emotions involved.

Be clear, conflict will not be effectively resolved if there is no facility for emotional release in conflict resolution.

Hence the South African Commission for Peace and Reconciliation.

4

Dealing with bosses who drive you barmy

> The brain is a wonderful organ: it starts as soon as you get up in the morning and doesn't stop until you get to the office.
>
> *Robert Frost*

People get promoted and become the boss for all kinds of reasons. Some do so because they are really good at what they do, manage people and situations well, have a good grasp of the wider picture and can communicate ideas easily. That's the boss from heaven. Unfortunately, many bosses are from hell!

- In technically oriented companies bosses are often promoted because they are anoraks and propeller heads. But, when it comes to people, they don't have a clue.
- In family businesses, they become the boss because their daddy says so.
- In corporations bosses get promoted because it is Buggin's turn – and they are Buggin.
- In some of the less attractive industries and public services, bosses who couldn't get a job anywhere else are common.

■ In sales environments successful sales people leave behind what they are good at, stop selling and make a mess of the detail needed to be a good boss.

■ In companies where there are problems, an accountant emerges as the boss.

■ In new, brave, IT and dot.com businesses, bosses are inexperienced and seldom good in a crisis.

Is there anywhere where a good boss can be found? Yes, of course there is. But it is worth making the point that bosses are not always promoted because they are good at being the boss. Being good at something, having good technical skills or having worked in an organisation for a long time is often the passport to having 'Boss' written on the door. For some, the job makes the man or woman. Others become walking nightmares.

Inside every poor boss is a voice that tells the boss he or she is a poor boss. So, what do poor bosses do? They compensate. They overcome their insecurity by becoming caricatures of what they think a boss should be. If no one has ever trained them in people management, workforce skills or dealing with human resources, how are they to know? So they make it up. They become arrogant, belligerent, they shout, scream and manipulate. They are difficult to please, selfish and insecure. And very easy to deal with!

First things first. They are the boss and they can show you the door. So if you quite like the idea of hanging on to your salary cheque at the end of the month, remember to be diplomatic. Let them feel they are in control – even if you are!

Mr angry

Work for Mr (or Ms) Angry? Easy. Let him get angry! What's it to you if he wants to have a tantrum? It seldom lasts for more than a few minutes. Let him boil over, erupt and explode. As long as you don't join in, you're safe. Even if you are 1,000 per cent right, have company policy, the law, the European Court of Human Rights and all the angels in heaven on your side, don't join in.

The trick is to make yourself scarce until it blows over. Here's what you do. Say:

> *I'm sorry you're so cross about this, but we need to deal with it rationally. I'm going to leave now and perhaps I can come back later when we've both had a chance to think it through.'*

Then leave. Whatever they say, leave. If he or she seems contrite, apologetic, even angrier, or wants you to stay – leave. If necessary, say 'No, *I want to leave it for now and perhaps I can come back in a hour or so and we'll look at it again.'*

Don't be tempted to have a row. It might be nice to fantasise about saying, 'You rude pig, how do expect anyone to work with you? All you do is fly off the handle.' But then you have another problem to deal with – where are you working next week? Stay cool and deal with the issue on your terms.

✓ TIP

The important word here is 'we'. It keeps you connected with events, shares the responsibility for what is happening and doesn't look like you are apportioning blame or being condemnatory. 'We' does nothing to inflame the situation.

Never let them see you sweat

Bully bosses like to see their staff sweat – so don't give them the pleasure. Whatever happens:

■ Stay calm.

- Don't scream back.
- Don't get into an argument. Don't tell them what to do with their job. *'Stick it where the sun don't shine'* may be very satisfying for 60 seconds but you'll regret it!
- And, never, never, never walk out on the spur of the moment.

 Think about this: why let a nightmare boss ruin a dream job?

✓ **TIP**

Bet you 20:1 this works...

This works. It really does. But I know you'll read this and groan. Trust me. It's the sort of advice your mother would give you and it works. It isn't magic, it isn't new and it isn't based on the latest psycho-fad. But, it is founded on the very good principles of stress and anger management.

Here it is: get away from the scene, row, punch-up, argument, or whatever. Get on your own and count backwards from 20 to 1.

Take a deep breath, concentrate and count: 20, 19, 18, 17, 16, 15, 14, 13, 12, 11, 10, 9, 8, 7, 6, 5, 4, 3, 2, 1.

For some reason counting upwards doesn't work. Counting backwards does. It has a calming influence. Ever seen a stage hypnotist at work? They always use the backward counting technique to relax their victims.

Actually, there are some very good psychological reasons why it does work, but now is not the time and place! When you next feel like the deputy prime minister, and giving an egg-chucker a straight left, try the 20 to 1 trick – odds on it will work for you.

When all else fails, what next?
OK, so you've done everything you can:

■ You've delivered everything on time.
■ When you couldn't deliver, you had a good reason and flagged up in advance that a deadline wasn't feasible.
■ You've supported your pig of a boss in public, never been abusive and never made him or her look a fool, even if he/she is.
■ You've worked with your boss, found out what gets him or her wound up and worked around it, over it and under it.
■ You've never given him or her any ammunition to shoot you with.

What next?
You could try mediation.

■ The human resource department may be able to help.
■ You could appeal to a more senior member of staff to help you.
■ You may even have said to your boss *'Look, I know we are all under a lot of pressure in this job and I can understand that means sometimes everyday niceties have to go by the board. However, I really don't think it is reasonable of you to expect me to put up with your behaviour and (describe a particular issue or incident so there is no ambiguity about what you are saying). We are going to have to find a better basis of working together.'*

In the end – what?
You only get one life and it is not (in a cliché worth a rerun) 'a rehearsal'. Leave, go, quit, get a life. If you are good at what you do, bale out and find another job. Do it on your terms, in your own time and at your own pace. Don't walk out, don't slam doors and don't threaten anything. Just leave. If you think

you have a case for an industrial relations tribunal, visit your local Citizen's Advice Bureau and find out. Leave quietly. Don't tell people you're looking for another job: there is no such thing as a secret. Don't be unhappy, life is too short.

Colleagues to throttle

One of the saddest things is that the only thing you can do for eight hours, every day, is work. You can't eat eight hours a day, nor drink for eight hours a day, nor make love eight hours a day.

William Faulkner

Open-plan offices, team working, group targets, syndicated bonuses. Shift working with hand-over responsibilities, production line manufacturing based on mutual performance. The direction of modern business is to have people working closer together – both physically and mentally. And spiritually for that matter!

Working with people means just that. It also means working, sometimes, with difficult people.

Very few of us have the luxury of being able to retreat into the solitude of our own office, shut the door and be quiet for a few minutes. For most of us the workplace is crowded, busy, bustling and often noisy. The canteen is just the same and the locker room is probably worse. The quietest place is probably the loo!

In open-plan offices, colleagues with booming voices are an irritation you can do without, and working in a stock-room with a colleague with BO is a job that stinks! Good workplace relationships are pivotal to company performance, and good managers and bosses understand that. The really good ones are not afraid to sort problems out – head on.

Managers often mistake the roll of competition within a company. Perhaps one of the best examples of an oxymoron comes from the management lexicon: 'friendly competition', a complete contradiction in terms. There is no such thing and it does not encourage performance. It does encourage intrigue, conspiracy, back-stabbing, and focuses attention on scoring rather than winning.

Collaborating to win and competing to beat companies in the outside world who are after your customers is a better recipe.

 Let's think about this

You can choose your friends, you can choose the neighbourhood you want to live in. You can choose where to spend your money and you can choose your partner. You can choose your job. The two things you can't choose are the two groups most likely to give you trouble! You can't choose your family and you can't choose your colleagues.

Got your head around that? So get it into perspective. Once you've come to terms with that, the rest is easy. Expect, from time to time, difficulties to arise. It would be a miracle if they didn't! If they don't, sit back and think how lucky you are.

✓ **TIP** Salespeople! Can there be a more difficult group of people in the whole universe? You're dealing with self-esteem, low self-esteem, arrogance, belligerence, pride, egoism, conceit, persistence, courage, confidence, perseverance, stamina and tenacity. A cocktail of just about every human emotion you can think of.

Then some fool comes along and says 'Motivate the sales team.' How? There is a group of men and women who are all in different stages of emotional and psychological disaster, highs and lows, peaks and troughs, complex home lives, personal disasters, challenges and happiness. It takes a brave fool to think there is a magic trick that will motivate 'the sales team'!

You could try this:

I once had the job of 'motivating the sales team'. It was a nightmare task to think up new ways of bribing them to perform better! They were a talented lot. Bright and no push-over. They enjoyed success, high incomes. Finding ticks to turn up performance got harder and harder.

One day, while ploughing my way through sales reports and numbers, I had a thought. On average the sales team would prospect 20 leads, make five solid appointments and close two sales. This meant we needed to get 18 people to say 'no' to get to the two that would say 'yes'.

I turned the whole reporting and reward system on its head. We encouraged people to get the 'no's. That way, the more 'no's we got, the closer we were to the next 'yes'. There was an interesting spin-off. The more fuss we made about 'no', the more interested the sales team became in talking about why prospects said 'no'. There was no longer any professional shame and nothing to hide about getting a 'no'. Techniques were analysed, sale presentation retuned and the product offering refined.

It really worked, and the prospect to close ratio doubled as we

Competition crazy

The modern business environment can produce the point-scoring competition-crazy colleague who drives everyone mad. You must have been in a meeting and heard 'I don't know what all the fuss is about. Our department did a project like that in half the time.' Or perhaps 'Our sales division always exceed targets like that.' Then again 'We regularly get through that amount of production in a third of the time.'

Ever been tempted to take the water jug and throw it over them?

Not a good idea. Try this instead: *'Yes, I know, and well done. But can we get back to this issue and talk about how we are going to deal with it.'* These few words – repeat them in identical form if you have to – will refocus the meeting, signal that everyone has moved on, and if the competition-crazy person comes back to their claim he or she will look very childish.

✓ TIP

Just give their ego a little polish and they'll sit back and glow. Easy. Works every time.

Rivals, antagonists and getting personal

Personal attacks don't work. They leave behind a stain on a relationship which can take forever to remove. People harbour grudges, bitterness and resentment, and these get in the way of the work that needs to be done.

Never let it get personal. Separate the issue from the person. Decouple the individual from the difficulty. Divide the personality from the problem.

Better not say *'Because of the way you've handled this, we are now in a real *%##^$ mess'*, even if it's true! All that will happen is that the individual will spend the next three hours defending him- or herself, his/her department, mother, family and the good Lord in heaven. It won't solve the problem. The problem is fixing the issue. So concentrate on the issue.

 Let's think about this

This 'don't let it get personal' approach is right out of the pages of so-called conflict resolution, a phrase you might have come across in connection with Northern Ireland. The past master of the approach is Sinn Fein leader Gerry Adams. He never gets personal and sticks to the issues like glue. You may not admire his politics but you have to admire his technique.

Try, *'We need to get this sorted, so let's look at (the issue) and agree the next step.'*

If someone tries to take the conversation back to whose fault it was, or goes down the road of name recrimination, bring them back on track fast. *'How we got into this situation is less important to us right now than seeing our way through it. Let's decide where we go from here.'*

It's always the quiet ones

Ever been in a meeting where some people sat still and said nothing? Ever wondered why? Are they shy? Perhaps they are embarrassed? Do they think they are too good for this place and you aren't worth bothering with? You know where you are with colleagues who blow their stack, are critical, or are keen to have a row. But where are you with the quiet ones?

Maybe they need a little confidence to get going. Perhaps they feel superior and don't want to intervene. It could be they need 'permission' to participate. It might be they are conspiring against you! (Included as an outside possibility, just to entertain the paranoid few!)

Whatever the problem, here's a way to coax them, get them going or smoke them out.

Ask for their opinion on a less important part of the overall topic. Simple questions that they will find easy to answer and look really stupid if they don't. Don't stop with one question. As the meeting progresses, ask them two or three questions, of a similar type.

Here's what will happen:

■ The shy ones will be coaxed into making a contribution.

■ The 'I am too good for this meeting' types will disdainfully answer the easy questions and will not be able to resist making a more high-powered intervention.

■ The conspirators will answer the question and stay quiet. Look out for them!

Staff to strangle

I should have worked just long enough to
discover I didn't like it

Paul Theroux

So, you've made it: you're somebody's problem boss. Well
done.

Now you have staff to die for, swing for and strangle. Ain't
being the boss fun? Well, it should be! In truth it's not easy.
Even though you are the boss, there will still be pressures on
you.

If you are a middle boss, then there will be pressure from
above. If you are a big boss, the chances are there will be a
bigger boss lurking someplace. If you are the boss of all bosses,
you'll still have shareholders, banks or the media to contend
with. No one gets off lightly in the modern world of business.

 Hazard warning

At the heart of every employee relationship problem I have ever
looked at lurked a 13-letter word:

Communication

Thirteen, got it? Unlucky for some – how about you?

In the annoying jargon of the management guru, all bosses have to *manage down* and *manage up*. Wouldn't your life be much easier if you didn't have to worry about the people? A business without staff – pure joy! (We'll get onto the customers later.)

Somehow you have to find a formula that maximises the productivity of the organisation and gets the best out of the staff you have – without being a slave driver or turning into a problem boss.

Communication and understanding are the ways to avoid dealing with difficult staff. Tell people what you want and expect from them, spell out how you want something done, and be clear about targets and objectives.

You'll hear this and more:

> ▓ You don't understand the pressures on the department.
> ▓ No one told me what the deadline for this order was. I thought next week would be OK.
> ▓ I didn't know you wanted it done differently, I always do it like that.

Didn't understand, no one told me, didn't know what you wanted: all too familiar? Afraid so. What's the answer? The first question is, do these staff failings make them 'difficult'? No. The problem is with the boss.

Here's a phrase to cut out and stick on the fridge door with one of those funny magnet things, or pin onto your notice board, or nail to your forehead:

No one ever ran a successful business sitting behind a desk.

While we're about it, here's another one:

If you don't take the time to tell people what you want, how do you expect they will ever be able to give you what you want?

And just for good measure:

If you always do what you always do, you'll always get what you've got.

 Let's think about this

The really world-class businessmen and -women in the UK are few and far between. The top-drawer ones all have something in common. They are fanatical about getting out and about in their businesses.

Lord Sieff built the world's best retailers, Marks & Spencer (yes, I know they may be approaching their sell-by date and they need a good shake-up to reflect the 21st century), by making sure he spent two days a week in the stores or at suppliers. Today Britain's best-known entrepreneur, Sir Richard Branson, is likely to turn up on one of his transatlantic planes, serving the drinks, or to sit next to you on one of his trains. He's also been known to serve customers in his record stores.

The guys who run the Carphone Warehouse show up at the shops. Rocco Forte, rebuilding his leisure empire, books into his hotels (under a pseudonym) several nights a week. All the top business people do it. They realise they have to, to understand the business, to find out what customers really want and how the staff go about their jobs.

In an effort to find out what it is like to be a patient in the NHS, Leicester NHS Trust puts trainee doctors in touch with patients with chronic conditions. They spend time with them and try to understand what it's like to be ill and frightened. They chaperone patients through accident and emergency departments and discover how awful it is to have to wait for hours to be attended to. They even stay in the homes of patients with long-term conditions, to understand the pressures there are on carers.

The BBC ran a fascinating series of programmes called *Back to the Floor*. Leading business types spent a week working on the 'shop floor' of their business. A grocer worked in the stores and on the checkout till. The owner of a chain of restaurants worked in the kitchens. The boss of a chain store worked on the shop floor, and the head honcho of a waste management company worked as a refuse collector.

They discovered a great deal about their business: little things, like not having enough room at a sales point to wrap the customer's purchases and faults in checkout procedures. The owner of the restaurants was so dismayed about working conditions and the attitude of the staff that he tried to pull out of the programme halfway through.

They all ended up with a much deeper understanding of their business, and each of them was able to introduce changes to make the lives of his or her employees easier.

By finding out what the business was really like, they were able to communicate with their staff on the basis of a good understanding of what could be achieved. They all decided that what they were getting was not what they wanted, and changed the way they did things.

By understanding your business, you'll have fewer 'difficult' staff and customers to deal with.

That's enough thinking – take a break. Take out your diary and mark off some days to spend in the organisation. I promise you, over time, you'll have fewer difficult people to deal with... or your money back!

Independent or stubborn?

Employees who solve problems, use their initiative and develop local answers to local problems are every good boss's dream. Encouraging operational independence is a great idea. But (sorry, there's always a 'but', isn't there?) when independence spills over into wilfulness and independence takes an employee off down a track of his or her own, it's time for the boss to act.

What to do? First ask yourself a question: why am I taking action?

- Is it because I can't get my own way?
- Is it because the member of staff is damaging the business by doing his or her own thing?
- Am I jealous that they found a better way and I feel undermined?
- Do I have a glorious dream that everyone has to be a team

player and I've got no time for individuals?
What is the real damage: your ego or the business process? You may have to accept that some staff, like Paul Anka's song, do it *My Way*. Is it screwing up the process, costing more than it should, affecting the productivity of the company, annoying other staff? Is it dangerous, putting people at risk? Or, is it a good idea you hadn't though of?

Think before you act. If you do, act with justification and right on your side. Remember, the rule book and the procedures manual may not be your best ally, especially if the wayward member of staff has genuinely found a better way.

However, when you do decide to sort out the problem, try to do it without destroying the motivation of your victim. *'I know you are used to doing it your way, but the company has good reasons for wanting you to do it another way. Let me take you through what they are.'*

At the end of the encounter, add this bit: *'We are really keen to learn from the experience of the people actually doing the job. If you can come up with a better/safer/faster/more reliable way, let me know and we'll see how it fits into the whole picture and try to implement it. We like good ideas.'*

That way your staff member may go home reassured in the knowledge they are not dealing with a difficult boss!

When the big hand gets to 12

Ever thought why staff become clock-watchers?

■ It could be they have problems at home.
■ Maybe they look after a sick partner or an elderly relative.
■ They may have to pick up their children from the crèche or childminder.
■ Perhaps they have to catch a train or bus.
■ Are they rushing off to evening classes or a secret assignation?

Who knows? You should! Shouldn't you? Leaving aside the assignation, shouldn't you know if your staff are under external pressure? Can you help? Change hours? Be a more family-friendly employer?

Perhaps there's another reason. Are they doing the job, or doing a good job of looking like they are doing the job? Could it be the job is mind-blowingly, eye-wateringly, brain-crunchingly dull, boring and depressing?

How do you judge them? Do they have potential? Do you want to give them a lift and motivate them? Of course you do. The modern workplace has refined and deskilled tasks to the point where work can be a drudge. Frequent breaks, swapping tasks and changing surroundings can all help to alleviate dreary jobs. Are you doing what you can?

How about giving this a try: *'I'd like to give you a change from the routine. Would you have a go at this for me...?'*

If it's not the work or the environment, the expectation is that it's personal.

✓ **TIP**

To remind of you what I said earlier, *'No one ever ran a successful business sitting behind a desk'*. If staff are under-motivated, clock-watching and performing poorly, how much of it can be attributed to the work, the working environment or the working methods?

Time to go back to the floor. Do the job yourself, find out what it's like. I'll bet real money that, in less than three days, you'll find a solution – or your money back!

Good bosses don't pry – but they should try

Loss of motivation, poor performance, lack of interest: which is it? There's only one way to find out. If you are satisfied it isn't a workplace issue, ask!

'I can see you're not getting much out of being at work these days. Is there something going on we can help you with?'

Expect the reply, 'No, nothing. I'm all right.'

'That's fine. I just wanted you to know that if there were something, my door is open and we can chat if you want to.'

You'll maybe get an answer, or a clue. Perhaps nothing. You may get an approach at a later time. Be patient. The important thing is, you've sent a signal, one that says, we'd be happier if you were happier. More than that you can't do.

 Take a well earned break. You tried your best.

Waving or drowning

Have you ever had high hopes for a member of staff, then discovered he or she just can't hack it? Ask yourself why.

▓ Was he or she recruited badly, with not enough research into career experience and background?
▓ Has the job shifted into more testing territory?

■ Has he or she got a personal problem that is on his/her mind?
■ Is he or she in debt?
■ Are his/her kids playing up?

Whatever it is, you're the boss. Dealing with difficult people and tricky situations is down to you. Get on with it!

Go back a page, or two, look for the coffee cup and read the bit above it. If it's a personal problem, the clue to dealing with it is in that section. If it's not, here are some options:

■ Do you need to organise some training?
■ Is the job too easy, so the individual is under-performing because he/she is not challenged?
■ Did the person give a false impression at interview, or was he/she perhaps untruthful about his/her experience?
■ Did referees lie?
■ Can you reorganise the process?
■ Can you shift some of the workload onto someone else for a while, to let the employee get up to speed?
■ Do you need to review your recruitment processes?

Next, talk to the person. Do it in the context of the original job interview.

■ Get out the paperwork.
■ Go over his/her experience and qualifications.
■ Take a view as to whether he or she should be coping better.

Agree training, or a respite period and a timetable for improvement. Review it regularly. If there is no real improvement, shift the individual to a less demanding role, or if you have to, let him/her go.

I'm sorry, but this isn't working out for either of us. Perhaps we should part company now to give you a chance to go for a job where you'll be more comfortable and we can be sure to get the work covered.

It's difficult, but kinder in the long run.

 Being a boss is not all glitz, is it?

When you've finished hitting people with the stick, try hitting them with the carrots.

Workplace rewards, bonuses, productivity payments, cash incentives are all part of the modern workplace. For some staff they are just right. When you say 'Jump', if the bonus is good enough, they'll ask, 'How high?'

Research shows that people work for more than money, and quite a high percentage of staff is not motivated by money.

This is particularly true of many public service workers who have a concept of principled motivation. They are driven by a service ethos and set great store by training opportunities and personal, professional development.

They are into something called pride-in-a-job-well-done. They're worried about the embarrassment or shame if they don't hit a target. Job satisfaction plays a big part in what motivates staff.

 Hazard warning

Don't expect to throw a big commission or bonus package into the office and expect everyone to grab it. Different people are motivated differently. That's what you call difficult!

Your expectations won't be the same as everyone else's. To make the carrot and stick work, try this:

■ Sit down with staff individually and explain the overall goal.
■ Agree the level at which the individual can make his or her contribution.
■ Be clear about performance levels and individual goals.
■ Encourage staff to stretch themselves, but being over-ambitious and setting unrealistic goals is no good for the company and very demotivating for the member of staff who fails to reach them.
■ Arrange regular sessions to monitor performance.
■ Be prepared to modify goals by mutual arrangement, but otherwise stick to the rules.

✓ **TIP**
Personal rewards are not always the answer. Some people are motivated by what they can achieve for others. Start with the family: days out, holidays as a reward for performance, make Mum or Dad look like real heroes at home and achieve more in motivation than even the best boss can.

Don't forget the possibility of linking performance to donations to a charity or other good cause.

Use the 'stick' to hold a person to his or her agreed objectives. Use the carrot to say well done.

Finding out how good a boss you've been

How's your back? Been stabbed lately? Unsuspecting bosses will have staff who are nice to their face and horrible the moment they are out of the office.

The first question is do you deserve it? Be honest with yourself: what sort of a boss are you? If you are satisfied you are not the boss from hell (if you are not sure, read the section at the beginning of the book. Recognise anyone?), then you'll have to act.

It is not just a personal thing. Staff who bitch about their bosses with no justification play hell with the reputation of the company and the morale of staff, especially junior members.

Feel that stabbing pain between the shoulderblades? Find a member of staff with a dripping bread knife. Try this:

What you think about me personally is up to you. However, we're not here for fun. There is a business to run and I do the best I can to run it. If you have a legitimate criticism of me, come and talk to me privately and directly. My door is open to you. Otherwise, keep your offensive remarks to yourself.

Tough? Yes, but that's why you're the boss. The other staff will soon realise what's happened and will probably be relieved they don't have to listen to the rubbish. More, you'll go up in their estimation for dealing with it.

Seriously difficult members of staff

This is not the book to teach you about employment law and industrial tribunals, but you do need to know your stuff, or know someone who does. That's why they pay you so much money!

Employment law is based on evidence. In recent years there have been huge shifts in the balance between the employee and the employer. This is good thing. No one wants to work in, or run, a sweatshop. The law is complex and a minefield for the unwary.

For operational purposes, the key phrases are: write everything down, keep contemporaneous notes, and hang on to evidence.

The golden rule is to deal with difficult issues as swiftly as you can. A rule that comes from the time-management gurus is good for those trying to deal with a difficult member of staff; make the job you least want to do your first job. Don't wait, don't let situations fester. Deal with it, no matter how difficult it is and no matter how reluctant you are and no matter how horrible it's going to be. Apply the JGDI rule: just go do it!

 Hazard warning

Employment law is stuff for experts. If you are a new boss, or a boss not sure of your ground, find out about company policy, talk to the human resources people and don't be shy about being ignorant. This is not the time or place for an enthusiastic amateur. If you are a self-employed boss, the Citizens Advice Bureau, the local job centre and books like Croner's *CCH Employment Law Manual* will point you in the right direction. If in doubt, ask a lawyer.

Massaging the egoist

One may understand the cosmos but never the
ego; the self is more distant than any star.

GK Chesterton

Successful people, to get where they are today, will have needed
a bit of luck, a lot of courage, some knowledge and generally a
great deal of effort.

They will be confident and they will be self-assured. They
will be proud of their achievements and they will be positive.
They are also likely to be egomaniacs!

Egoists, show-offs, the self-centred, the know-alls; or the
insecure, the easily flattered and the attention seeker. It's not
difficult at all. They're all easy to deal with.

If the difficulty is an egomaniac boss

It's easy: give the boss the credit! All right: not all the time. But
you don't have to take the credit every time, do you? If you
want to get your own way with an egoist, flattery is the easy
way to do it. Got a great idea that you want to get past your
egomaniac boss? Try this:

I've read the memo you sent out about reorganising the western division. You know, I think you're right. Taking what you said as the foundation, here's what I thought we might do...

Can you possibly get away with that? You certainly can! Egoists are blind. If you and the egomaniac boss stand side by side and look into a mirror – the boss will only see themselves.

✓ TIP

You'll never change the boss but you can change how people think about you.

Does this sound like giving in, giving up or rolling over? Only if you're no good at your job. Egomaniac bosses can be seen (and enjoyed) by all the employees, not just you. If you are good at what you do and shine, pretty soon everyone will know where the good ideas are coming from, so don't worry about one-upmanship.

If the difficulty is an egoist working for you

If you are trying to get a group of people to work together, behave as a team and develop a close-knit motivation, the last thing you want is an egomaniac grabbing the headlines for him- or herself. Give this a try:

Eleanor, I know you are working very hard and doing your best for us, but I am anxious to get everyone up to a high performance standard. I want you to make sure everyone gets their share of the credit. That way we all do better. Don't you agree?

Getting Eleanor the egoist onside is easy. Just appeal to her ego: ask for a little help to spread the praise.

The egomaniac colleague

Mr Perfect, Miss Right: mistake! But that's their problem. The solution is to listen to them boast and puff themselves up and then stick to the facts. Don't prick their bubble, just let them down slowly. Sticking to the facts and figures will do that for you. '*Well done. Just how many/how much did you actually do to achieve whatever...?*' No matter what they say, you've sent a signal. Loud and clear you are saying that you're not interested in the bull, you're interested in the meat. They will soon stop boasting if they know you are the type of person who will want the facts to back up their bragging.

Knocking the know-all

This is tricky: remember, you have to work with these people! 'Shut up, you big-headed bitch' does it, but doesn't do it – if you know what I mean. Think of this like a judo throw. Judo players know they won't get anywhere by pushing and shoving. They wait for their opponent to push and then they pull, using the momentum of their rival. Don't try to beat an egoist at their own game. Make them play yours.

Be like the judo player: train hard. Or in this case, get the facts and go for it: '*I'm not sure you're being quite accurate there, Edward. I've had a look at the records and actually...*' Edward and his ego nicely fall flat on their backs. Don't try to out-ego the egoist and don't try to beat up him or her. Just go for the facts and let them do the work.

Egoists are easy to put down. Just deny them the oxygen of attention and they will wither away. Is that what you want? If the idea is to get the best out of people, the odd compliment, the occasional pat on the back and some recognition once in a while should keep them on the team and make the situation manageable.

Handling aggressive people without getting thumped on the nose

Nobody ever forgets where they buried the hatchet.

Hubbard

Let's define our terms. This is not about learning Aikido or Japanese kick boxing. Neither is it about selecting which jungle knife to take into the office. Workplace bullies and aggression that ends up in fisticuffs need to be sorted out by the police, the law, industrial tribunals and not you.

This is about the kind of aggression the masks performance or hides bad behaviour. Sometimes tactless people can appear aggressive, as can the sarcastic. They have the sort of 'gets under your skin' behaviour that begs you to plant a left hook.

This is not the time or place for a dissertation on psychiatry. The seeds of this sort of behaviour can be deeply planted, so let's not spend time trying to dig them up. What is needed is to achieve what you want to achieve and move forward.

Be clear about your objectives, get the facts on your side and look for outcomes to measure.

Aggression takes on several guises. Hypocrisy, condescension, double-dealing, sabotage, bullying, set-ups, unwarranted criticism, delegation to the point where you are snowed under: they are all there somewhere.

One answer is to perform out of your socks, stick to the facts and hope pretty soon the boss will recognise what's going on.

 Let's think about this

Aggressive folks are often very critical. Be sure not to reject criticism out of hand. They might be right.

Criticism from customers must be listened to. Criticism from junior colleagues is worth attending to: think how much courage it has taken for them to face you.

If you can get to the mind-set where criticism is as valuable to you as a compliment, you've cracked it.

If an aggressive manager is trying to dump on your ideas

They'll try to drown you in details, suffocate you with demands for statistics. They'll pulverise you with planning, more planning and re-planning, terrify you with tales of how it will never work and the terrible consequences. Try this. See if it is possible to downsize your idea, be less ambitious:

Could we pilot the idea for a couple of months, in one territory and see how it goes? We can evaluate it and see if it is worth rolling out across the rest of the area later.

If you're landed with a project that will never fly

One sneaky tactic of the aggressive manager is to dump you with a project that will never work and let you take the blame for failure. Try to widen the number of people who could end up looking stupid.

> *Goodness knows why we've ended up with this. It's obvious that it's a no-hoper. Everyone is going to look stupid, finance, corporate, production and middle management. Shouldn't we get together and decide what we're going to do?*

✓ TIP

Does anyone else feel the same as you? Have a quiet word with trusted colleagues; *'Maybe it's just me but, I think Andrew is very aggressive and I find it very daunting to deal with. How do you feel?'*
Find some allies and deal with the problem together.

If you're being stabbed in the back

This is the favourite ploy of the aggressive manager or colleague. Thought you had their support? Thought they were behind you? Well, they were, at least until there was a problem. Now, they've disappeared.

What next? Clever, calculated and cunning confrontation is called for! *'I thought we had agreed our approach here and that there were five things we needed to do. I remember we talked about it.'* The person is bound to say, 'No, I never signed up to any of that.' It's time for some salvage. *'Look, there is no point in arguing about it. Let's sort out what we can agree on and move on. How about this and this and this?'*

✓ TIP

Don't be caught out twice. This kind of behaviour is very hard to stop in its tracks. Be prepared to work around it. First rule: make notes. When you have a planning meeting, formal, or informal, make notes. If there are no formal minutes, make your own notes. Date them and keep them. Next time there is a problem: bingo! Produce your notes. It will make the stabbers and the hypocrites think twice before they mess with you again.

9

Putting a bomb under the lazy ones

He has his law degree and a furnished office. It's just a question, now, of getting him out of bed.

Peter Arno

No one ever made a donkey go faster by hitting it with a stick. Well, maybe they did, but carrots do usually work better.

Why do people get lazy? Are they born idle? Some are. We know work can be routine, monotonous, tedious and uninteresting. Employees who start out being diligent and productive can be hypnotised into inactivity, simply by the nature of what they are doing.

Re-engineer the task, change the approach and let the staff, if you can, have a big say in the working environment and the way they approach it.

Don't be afraid to challenge lazy-bones:

Justin, you seem to be having a lot of problems getting your projects finished on time. You know we have to depend on you delivering. What can we do to make you more reliable?

The subtlety here is to turn the criticism into a question. 'Why are you always late delivering?' is designed to invite a whole load of excuses, waffle, rebuttal and aggravation. 'You seem to be having trouble, what can we do about it?' focuses the energy in a different direction and invites a more positive response.

Hazard warning

Whose fault is it anyway? Are the staff lazy or poorly managed? You wont get five-star performance if people don't know what they are supposed to be doing. Have you given clear instructions? Is what you are asking realistic? Is there any confusion about what is expected?

Clock-watchers, rule-bookers and not invented here

This is about motivation: making people tick faster than the clock. Have a good look at the way people are working. If you can, spend some time doing the job yourself. That way you'll have a good idea what's wrong and what you can do about it.

What can you change? The environment? The process? The times? The schedules? The materials? The tools? The equipment? The breaks? The clothing? The music? Wherever you can, involve the lazy lot. Introduce ideas to engage staff:

■ team-based solution meetings;
■ team bonuses;
■ group quality initiatives;
■ rotating jobs.

Do the staff see the whole process or do they just see 'their bit' of the production? Widen their interest by opening up the whole process. Do the staff ever talk to the customer or end-user of the process or service?

When the importance of their role in the process is emphasised, staff often find a new motivation.

If you are held back by an idle colleague

Change your colleague is the simple answer! If only life were that simple.

You can rarely choose who you work with, and if you are teamed up with idlers, dawdlers or day-dreamers life can be pretty miserable.

Are they just disorganised? Can you get them better organised? Help them to time manage. Lead by example. Getting into the detail may help. Prepare a detailed list or schedule, review points and outcome measurements. Make sure they understand the delivery points, what they have to do and what part they are playing. Use milestones to move your millstone. If all else fails:

Janet, I really want to get this project delivered on time. We are running late and I'm still waiting for your work/production/input. Shouldn't we sit down together and make a timetable that we can both live with and be sure of delivering?'

> ## ✓ TIP
> Got a colleague who is always late? Start without them. Ignore them. When they arrive, make them catch up. They'll soon learn.

A boss who loiters

Delays, dithering, procrastination, stalling, dawdling? Putting decisions back into the in-tray? Why do they do it? Infuriating, isn't it? There are a lot of reasons why bosses don't cut the mustard. They may be out of their depth. They may be short on some information. They may not have the same priorities as you. The answer is to help them out. Do they need some background work, some research, someone to be a gofer?

There's the answer. Do it for them. Help to make making the decisions easier. This may mean more work, but to get a project moving and finished it might be worth looking at your extra work as an investment.

Do it right and don't expect to be thanked. Bosses with too much to do, out of their depth and drowning will seldom admit it. To find an employee who is prepared to do the extra bit, go the extra inch, yard or mile, is to find salvation.

Be subtle and get it right and you become indispensable. You also run the risk of being put-upon, dumped on and exploited. Your call...

Hazard warning

Take care not to overstep your authority.

Don't make the decision, just line up the facts and figures so that the decision can be made with the minimum of effort and risk.

How you eat an elephant

American management guru Tom Peters, in his book *In Pursuit of Excellence*, gives us the answer: elephant burgers, elephant steak, elephant stew, elephant risotto, elephant kebab. Get the idea?

If people are swamped by the size of the task they will often withdraw, dawdle, procrastinate and get to look (and be) lazy.

The answer is to break the job up into bite-size segments, and agree and set priorities and deadlines. Stay in touch and on top of the project, and be ruthless in insisting deadlines are met.

Look out for employees who delight in appearing swamped, overworked and with an in-tray that would take 10 strong men to lift. They are probably not lazy. When they are waving for attention it probably means they are drowning. Help them, teach them to prioritise. Rip this out and stick it on the notice board in the office:

Success by a yard is hard. Success by an inch is a synch.

The criminally lazy

They have 'lazy' to an art form. They will whine, plead, grizzle, moan, conspire and devote the energy it takes to run 10 power stations to avoid doing the job.

Treat them like any other criminal: *'Sorry Ronnie, I'm up to my arm-pits in my own stuff, you're on your own.'*

 Let's think about this

It takes a lot of energy to be lazy, keep a job and not get caught. It needs planning, forethought, charm, effort, energy, determination, intelligence, originality, guile and judgement: all the things needed for success and to be a five-star employee.

Perhaps there are no lazy staff, just bad bosses?

10

Beating the bullies at their own game

There is nothing ignoble in loving one's enemies
– but there is much that is dangerous.

Bernard Levin

Let's face it, Attila the Hun got things done. Genghis Khan went places. Working for either of them wasn't exactly a bowl of cherries.

Bosses do think (or some bosses do) that the best boss is the boss who shouts the loudest, slams the doors and frightens everyone out of their wits.

They see TV bosses shouting and read about pulp fiction bosses who leap off the page and grab staff by the short and curly bits.

Tyrants want a fight and bullies love a victim. There's the clue in what to do with a bully for a boss. Don't fight and don't be a victim.

Bullies become bullies because they find they can get away with it, and bullies are bullies because they have no other management technique. Lack of skills, insight, insecurity and incompetence turns bad bosses into bully bosses.

Let's think about this

If bullies need a victim, why are you a victim? You need a job? Sure, we all do. You need to pay the bills? Yup, of course. But you only have one life, so don't spend it in fear.

If you've tried everything and life is still hell, what next?

Shouldn't you be taking your time and quietly, subtly and decisively looking for another job?

The decibel dictator

How do you deal with the screamer, the abuser, the table thumper? Stay calm, unemotional and objective.

I know you are concerned about this, and of course it needs to be sorted out, but shouting at me (abusing me) is not going to solve the problem. It is very unsettling and upsetting and won't make me work any better.'

Very straight to the point.

What next? The boss will need a way to climb down, so expect a follow-up tirade of less intensity and of the self-justification type: 'Just as long as you understand the importance of all this... blah, blah.'

Answer, *'I do, so let's concentrate on the issues. What is the first step?'*

When you can't do anything right

Made a foul-up? Admit it, don't fudge it, apologise and offer to work to put things right. That's common sense. Are you being wrongly accused? Then try, '*You need to know the following three facts. The work is not completed because 1..., 2..., 3...*'

When all else fails

The boss has lost it. The screaming can be heard in mainland Europe and the rest of the staff have run for cover. What do you do? Cower, hide, cringe, tremble, quake, shrink? Go to the boss's boss? That's risky.

Stabbing with the office staple-gun? A crack on the head with a ruler? Electrocution with a badly wired keyboard? Sounds very satisfying, but you're likely to end up in jail and the bully isn't worth the best years of your life.

 Bully bosses often mimic behaviour. They get it from their boss.

If your boss's boss is a bully, the chances are your boss will be a bully. It'll be accepted behaviour and part of the organisation culture, so appealing to a higher authority is likely to prove an unfruitful tactic.

What to do? In truth, find another job and let some other mug take the flack. You don't need it. You're too good.

Stay as calm as a cucumber and try this. '*Mr Bulstrode, sit down/still and think.*' I'll bet Bulstrode will shut up (or your money back). Continue, '*You are upset and I can see why, but you have no right to talk to me like that (use that language/say those things). If you want to continue this, talk to me in a civil way and we can sort out the problem.*' Then say nothing, look as neutral and unflustered as you can and wait. Bulstrode will have to back off.

Don't stay and be the victim. Get out of the firing line, and do it without blame, accusation or reproach. Say 'Brian, I'll see you later', and clear off. Get out of there. Bullies need victims and audiences.

✓ TIP

The worst thing you can say to someone who has lost it is 'Calm down'. They'll scream back at you, 'I am calm!' Try to major on the issues and not the behaviour.

The firework colleague

What lights their touch-paper? One minute they're cuddly and workable-with, the next they are a Chinese firecracker. Can you detect what sets them off? If you can, keep off the topic, or issue. When the fireworks start, obey the four golden rules:

- Don't accuse – it adds fuel to the fire.
- Don't say things like 'Calm down' – it'll exacerbate things.
- Don't join in – you'll prolong it.
- Don't stay in the firing line – it's not safe.

When the dust settles, don't get into recriminations. Move on: '*I know this is important. Let's sort it out together because together we're more likely to succeed.*'

Let's think about this

Feeling intimidated? If you are feeling intimidated, the chances are you are being intimidated. This kind of fear is insidious. Ask yourself why you're feeling intimidated. Do you feel insecure, inadequate, not up to the job, got something to hide? How we react to people starts within ourselves. If we want to be a victim, then we will be. If we let people push us around, they will.

If you are on top of the job, doing the best you can, you have no reason to feel intimidated. Don't expect logic to play an part in this human relations equation. Bullies are not logical, they are opportunistic and unpredictable. Your defences are your talent, skill, patience and coolness under fire. Avoid the emotions and stick to the facts. Stay away from the passion and follow a plan.

11

Moaners, groaners and critics

Pay no attention to what the critics say. No statue has ever been put up to a critic.

Jean Sibelius

In a perfect world we'd all be perfect and there would be nothing to moan about, nothing to grumble about and nothing to criticise. As it stands, it is not (yet) a perfect world, things will go wrong, there will be foul-ups, mistakes and blunders. So expect moaners, groaners and critics.

Constructive criticism, delivered with sincerity and in the spirit of doing things better, is no bad thing. Some bosses take it too far, mainly because they're not very good at being a boss. But then who is?

If you are stuck with a critical boss, your best defence is to stick with the facts. If they grumble, produce the notes, the memos, the work, the invoice, the plan, the meeting minutes. Like the man in the US detective television programme used to say, 'Stick to the facts, ma'am.'

Overly serious bosses can fall into the trap of taking great performance for granted and majoring on the times when things go wrong. Don't be the wrong sort of boss. Try not to be too overly!

If the facts don't come out on your side, admit the mistake, offer to put it right and agree a course of action to make sure it doesn't happen again. If you've got a grizzly boss and you know there is a foul-up, the best advice is to get in first. Be proactive and confess:

> I'm not really sure how this happened, and we'll have to look into it to find out, but the Williams account is late on delivery. May I suggest we take the following action to put it right, look into how it happened and make some arrangements to ensure that this type of thing is not overlooked again. I'm really sorry.

This may not save you from a roasting but it might save you from getting fired.

Cold water torture

It's not just bosses who can be a pain. Colleagues can consistently try to trash your great ideas. Try getting them onside by having a private word. You'll get to know the kind of thing that makes them turn negative; think about it and add it to the equation. Work around the negativity. Negative people are often insecure people who are not inventive and not creative. In the face of inventive people and creative types they feel their own limitations and try to make up for the difference by stamping all over your ideas. Try sharing your ideas with them. Get them onside by offering co-ownership of a project you want to get through.

Try building alliances, coalitions and connections

Peddle your ideas around colleagues, ask for opinions, champions and white knights. Get friends onside and positive feedback before involving the grumpy one. Be sure to reveal your idea when your supporters are present. The moaners and the groaners often disappear when they find they have no allies.

Let's think about this

Not keen on the idea of sharing the idea? Is it better to give away some of the praise to get the idea off the ground? Sharing the credit might make the idea fly.

Words you don't want to hear

'Nothing like that can be done.' Try, *Oh dear, I'm sorry to hear that. Tell me why you say that. How can you be sure this particular plan won't work?*

'We tried that before and got into a real mess.' '*Yes, I know. I looked at the Mark II project and have been careful to avoid the pitfalls that trapped that team. Let me explain how this is different.*'

'Why do we need to bother with all that?' '*This approach saves money/time/effort/makes a better widget/is faster/more thorough. (Sell the benefits.) Let me explain how…*'

'We don't do things like that here.' '*I know we don't, but I think we should start. Let me explain why.*'

When critics turn the gun on themselves

Criticism is contagious. Add an organisation's capacity to create gossip and you're soon dealing with an epidemic. If the criticism is well founded, don't be precious, take it on board and deal with it, and let everyone know you've done so. Otherwise, try to get the arch-critic on board. *'Damon, I know you'll have some strong opinions on this, so before I go public I want to have your views.'* Approaching it this way gives you two chances. First, you'll know what the arguments will be and you can prepare. Second, you might just end up with an ally.

Staff with little confidence will often be self-critical. They seem to think it's easier if they criticise themselves before someone else does. If you're the boss and have staff members like that, you must act.

Staff are any organisation's most important asset. It is vital they are motivated, confident and encouraged. Take them to one side and say:

It is a great shame to hear you talking like that. You have excellent skills/experience/energy/enthusiasm/loyalty... and I hate to hear you waste it. You're doing a good job. See, I've told you. Now tell yourself.

 Let's think about this

Staff may put themselves down in the hope that someone will come along and tell them how great they are at their job. Don't get suckered into that one. Stick with *'I think we both know what sort of job you're doing. If I didn't think you were good enough, you wouldn't be in the department/on the team, so let's stick to the facts.'*

12

Perfectionists can be a pain

American women expect to find a perfection in
their husbands that English women only hope to
find in their butlers.

Somerset Maugham

Successful organisations need all types of personalities to make
them work. Getting a job finished, a design completed or a
project concluded generally depends on the input of the perfectionist, the master of detail – perhaps even the hyper-fussy. To
the extrovert the perfectionist can be excruciating company.
The fact is, we need them.

It's when the hyper-fussy becomes the nit-picker, inflexible,
rigid and obstinate, that we have a difficult person to deal with.
Sticklers for detail often won't realise they are being difficult.
From their perspective, detail, rules and regulations are the
things that glue organisations together.

They will hide a lack of vision or creativity behind a process,
sometimes the law, and always a file of memos and notes.

Why should there be a section in a book about difficult
people that is dedicated to perfectionists? In a world of rushing
around and doing things half-cocked, shouldn't we try and find
a few more perfectionists?

My answer is yes and no! We need the perfectionist's commitment to fine detail and the small print; we can use them to keep us on the straight and narrow. But we can do without the perfectionist's narrow focus, inflexibility and turgid obsession with the rules and regulations. We need to loosen them up a little:

> *How you deal with all this detail is a mystery. Still, it's a good job someone around here does. But the truth is, on this project we have a tight turnaround time and a lot of effort going into delivery. This time I'm not too worried about the details, we just need to push it along.*

That might work better than '*You pedant, can't you see you're holding the whole process up.*'

 Hazard warning

To beat perfectionists at their own game is to commit yourself to perfection. Is what you do as good as it can be? Is it as good as it could be?

There's no point taking on a perfectionist from anywhere but the moral high ground. They might even come to admire you as a kindred-spirit.

What turns on a perfectionist

Surprisingly, not the detail, not the books of measurements and the rules. They thrive on a strong sense of accomplishment and achievement. They have high personal standards, which are often their undoing. They are so fixed on getting it right, they lose sight of the big picture. Constantly focusing them on the big picture and the part they play can loosen them a little.

Peter, if you carry on checking the measurements three times/cross-checking the ledger entries/auditing the software more than once, we'll not only run over budget but we'll miss the delivery date. What can you do to help us?

✓ TIP

Perfectionists can get lost in their own world and lose all track of time and schedule. Help them with a course on time management. Teach them to break work into sections and set deadlines for each segment. That way they will enhance their sense of achievement, having delivered the goods and to a deadline.

Rules are rules

Every organisation has to have rules. Without them there is chaos. However, modern business thrives on origination and spontaneity. Can you be creative within the rules? Yes, you can, but sometimes you have to be creative with the rules.

Soldiers follow the rules and their orders, but most outstanding acts of bravery and courage have taken place against a background of no rules, or the rule book being thrown out of the window. A modern manager is nothing if not creative.

The perfectionist needs to be given permission to be less than perfect:

Peter, you know what we've budgeted for this and I don't want to go any higher. However, we must get delivery on time and with less than 1 per cent quality rejects. If that means we have to sensibly negotiate on the price, so be it. I'll trust your judgement and I know you will use it well.

Let's think about this

Perfectionists who know their stuff can be real pains or great resources: your call!

The perfectionist boss

They expect long hours, commitment, blood, sweat and tears. Delegate parts of the job if you can. If it gets too much, say so:

Boss, I know how much store you set by accuracy and delivery, but there is just too much on for me to promise to give either, or perhaps both. Can we talk about breaking the job up or getting some more help?

13

Manipulating the manipulators

Calamities are of two kinds: misfortune to ourselves and good fortune to others.

Ambrose Bierce

When does management become manipulation? What's the difference between motivation and manipulation? When does manoeuvring become manipulating? The dictionary gives us a clue:

> **manipulate** /me'nipj Ω,leit/ v.tr 1 handle, treat or use, esp. skilfully 2 manage to one's own advantage, esp. unfairly or unscrupulously

There's a bit more about manipulating text on a computer, and a reference to manually examining, but 'manage to one's own advantage, especially unfairly or unscrupulously': that's about what we're looking for.

In the modern workplace, how can you avoid it? It's dog eat dog out there, but when motivation, management and manoeuvring become unfair we have to do something.

The first rule is, don't try to out-manipulate a manipulator. Instead, deal with it head on. To do otherwise moves you into the complex world of conspiracy, plotting and scheming. Anyway, you haven't got time. Deal with the difficulty and move on.

Being manipulated by the boss? That's tricky. Try this: *'Boss, I know you are a fair person, but what you've decided here has caused me a real problem.'* Appealing to his or her better nature is more likely to pay off than complaining about the manipulation.

If you're being lined up to take the blame

The classic! Your boss, a colleague, even one of your staff, is looking for a fall guy. Hands up who has not come across this scenario.

A project has gone pear shaped and everyone is looking for somewhere to dump the blame. Unfortunately, at the outset of the project, in your normal cheery, optimistic way you said (or worse, wrote in an e-mail) that you thought it looked like a flyer, a great idea. Three months later – crash...

Suddenly, out of a clear blue sky, it was 'your project', 'your fault' and 'down to you'. Ugh! What next?

You could try *'You're not seriously suggesting all this is down to me, are you?'* Wriggle, squirm!

I doubt that will be enough. Here's a better suggestion:

There were 14 of us involved in this and two main departments. True, it did look OK to me at the outset, but there were a lot of other people involved, including the regional management. Hindsight is a wonderful thing. Perhaps we'd all do better if we stopped laying blame and started building some solutions.

That's a much better approach and shows that up with the

blame you will not put. Either you all go down, or you all sort it out.

The important thing here is to get this rebuttal up and running fast. That way you avoid being suffocated in the inevitable gossip that surrounds a juicy corporate cock-up.

Lies are manipulations and they don't always come in the big black wriggling form. They can be white lies, half-truths and part of selective omissions. However you wrap it up, if it isn't the truth, the whole truth and nothing but the truth, it's dangerous.

Hazard warning

Liars are one step up from manipulators, and it is not a very big step. People who manipulate not just colleagues but the truth as well are easy to deal with. Just stick to the facts, the records, the minutes and the data. Oh, and don't call anyone a liar. As far as you are concerned they are confused, uninformed, not up-to-date and have perhaps taken their eye off the ball. Let the others call them a liar. That way you make allies, not enemies.

Deal with a half-truth as if it was an oversight or an error. The liar will know what you are doing and everyone else will think you're on the ball. *'Lawrence, what you are saying is right, but I think you forgot to mention that the client said they wanted the blue colour in the first batch.'* Avoid being judgemental. *'Lawrence, you left out the client preference from your report. Did you do that to make my department look daft?'* It might be true but it creates friction and aggravation. Just be ready with the facts.

Let's think about this

Isn't it strange how often difficult situations and difficult people are neutralised by the facts? I bet you're pleased you keep notes!

Let's do a deal

This could be the chance of a lifetime, or you could be being manipulated. Your call! You'll have to do the deal to find out. It is a reasonable assumption that the people you are dealing with are honest, but if the deal looks too good to be true, it probably is. Remember, the key to doing a deal is that everyone gets something out of it. Figure out the deal from your side, sure, but more importantly, think about the deal from the other side of the table. What's in it for me? What's in it for them? If it looks like the deal is all on your side, look again!

Verbal promises aren't worth the paper they're not printed on! Manipulators see themselves as deal-makers. If the trade-off involves you promising to do something that is dependent upon someone else doing something, what happens if they don't? Are you stuck, stranded and looking sheepish?

The first golden rule: if it's right for the project, do it. If in doubt, don't.

The second golden rule: doing deals calls for records, minutes and agreements. They don't have to be formal:

The purpose of this memo is to record my understanding of what was agreed at the meeting on 31/02/03. John agreed to do this, I agreed to do that, and the whole thing will be delivered by...

This might be just enough to do the trick. The purpose is not to have a piece of paper to wave in the high court, but to flag up to any would-be manipulator that you're on the ball and not a pushover.

If you're easily flattered

You gorgeous creature! Of course you are. We all are! Ever heard anything like this: 'You are so good at PowerPoint slides, would you make a set for my presentation tomorrow? And there you are, up until the small hours creating a masterpiece. Manipulated by a master. You should have tried:

> *Mary, thank you for your kind words, but I find giving a presentation is a personal thing, and you'll be more confident and give a better presentation if you compose the slide-show yourself. If you want to run them by me when you've finished, I'd be happy to help out with the finishing touches.*

Now you can spend the evening doing what you want to do.

 Hazard warning

If you think you're being manipulated or bounced, you probably are. Good manipulators will go to any length to disguise what they do in flattery and compliments. Trust your instincts. If it doesn't feel right, don't wear it. Dig a bit deeper and ask some questions. Why, when, who, what and where are a few starters.

If you're flattered by your staff

You know you are the dream boss, and once in a while it's nice to be told that you are. But beware of flatterers who use their charms to get you to give them the easy jobs or to overlook their shortcomings. Try, *'Sylvia, thank you. It's nice to be appreciated but I think we should get on with the job.'*

Flattery, sycophancy, boot-licking, toadyism: none of it is very nice and you can do without most of it. Beware too of the personal undertones that might accompany flattery. Workplace problems include accusations of inappropriate behaviour and falling foul of the 'politically correct' police. If it looks like there could be a problem, confide in your boss. If you are the boss, talk to a senior member of staff or a lawyer.

14

Shifting the stubborn

Human reason only has to will more strongly that fate.

Thomas Mann

When the immovable object is met by the irresistible force, expect a bang. People who are set in their ways, obstinate, dogged and contumacious: don't you just love them!

There is just about one lever to try. Use a fulcrum point called 'the facts'. In most circumstances it is about as powerful an ally you could have. For shifting the stubborn, it's magic.

Sharon, I know you don't like using a different releasing agent, but I've come across this test report about a new line. It is 5 per cent more powerful, comes in a much more convenient storage container and is 10 per cent cheaper. Do you think we should get a sample delivered?

✓ TIP

Still having trouble shifting the stubborn? Try recruiting some allies. Put yourself in a position to be able to say, *'Sid, I've shown this to just about everyone I can think of in sales, production, marketing and accounts, and they all agree it's a good idea. I'd be grateful if you could find the time to give me your opinion.'*

Is someone being stubborn because he or she is embarrassed? Is he or she trying to hide a failure or foul-up? Is he or she unable to cope with a change in working practices? Is he or she out of his/her league? *'Derek, I know you're digging your heels in over this and it's not like you. Is there an issue I'm not aware of?'* Before giving someone a task, it's worth being absolutely sure he or she is comfortable with what you are asking him or her to do: *'This is big task and I want to be sure you're happy to take it on.'*

When the customer knows best

Got a stubborn customer? Insisting they want a product of a certain type when you know it's not going to do the job? How honest are you? Are you a gambler? If you do the right thing, you could end up losing the sale or making a friend for life. Ready for a gamble? Try this:

> Mr Witherspoon, I'm in business to sell things, and if you want the Mark IV, I'll sell it to you. But I know the kind of performance you're looking for means the Mark IV will overheat and burn out in three months. The Mark VIII is designed for the type of work you are doing, and I'd be happier to sell you that. Would you like me to show it to you?

You've done all you can!

15

Morale, attitude and how was it for you?

If you feel depressed you should not go out –
because it will show on your face. Misery is a
communicable disease.

Martha Graham

My starting point for this section is that there is only one
person who can affect my morale and that person is me.

I guess everyone is not like me, and a good thing too, I hear
you say! In the real world, the workplace, your organisation,
there will be pressures, changes and events that will impact on
people's attitude to work. Corporate morale is a difficult thing
to judge. We are told morale is at rock bottom in public
services, yet I can introduce you to inspired teachers, devoted
nurses and brilliant doctors. How do you measure morale, and
how do you know when it is on the downward run? Look for
the signs:

- There are more flash-points and arguments between
  staff.
- Sickness and unplanned absence levels rise.

- Groups 'circle the wagons', and cliques and informal groups appear.
- Gossip is rife and rumours are spread.

What to do?

Chapter 8 deals with flashpoints and anger. Rows and arguments that result from poor morale have to be dealt with in the same basic way, but there is a subtlety. Dealing with a normal row means finding out what the causes of the problem are and dealing with the row and the causes.

Disputes that arise out of poor morale follow the same rules, but the cause of the row is often much more difficult to ferret out.

When someone is having a screaming match use the three-step technique:

- Acknowledge their anger.
- Then ask a question.
- Finally, repeat back to them what they have said.

The conversation will go something like this:

You: *'I can see, Alan, you're very angry. This is not like you. What's upsetting you?'*
Alan: 'Nobody ever listens to a word I say.'
You: *'OK, you're saying no one listens to you. Well, I'm listening now. What do you want to tell me?*

The next step is the crucial bit. You have to listen! Ask more questions and listen again. At the bottom of the anger, you'll find the reason: gossip about redundancies, changes in working practices making the job more difficult to do, the need for more modern equipment, unexpected work-load. It will be there somewhere.

If you're sick of the sick

An otherwise healthy staff member who suddenly starts to have a poor sickness record is a sure sign something is wrong. Whatever is wrong is unlikely to be put right in the doctor's surgery. The telltale signs are absences either side of a weekend or public holiday. Friday and Monday absences, linked with claims of sickness, are worth looking out for.

Poor morale, lack of motivation, listless performance and a poor sickness record go hand in hand.

Action? Confront the sickness without being intrusive:

Sheila, I've noticed you've had (number of days) off with sickness in the last quarter/month. I'm concerned about you. Are you a bit 'under the weather' or is there something wrong that I can help you with?

Bringing the sickness record to attention is often enough to change a pattern of behaviour.

Do you have access to occupational health services? If you do, you can refer an employee with a sudden decline in healthy days for an opinion. However, don't expect the doctor or nurse to reveal the details of an employee's health: that's confidential. And don't expect the clinicians to do the manager's job of getting a lead-swinger back to work. They can tell you that a member of staff is generally healthy enough to do the job they are hired to do, and they will help an employee with any health problems they come across. That's all.

Everyone having a sickie

Poor morale can lead to endemic lead-swinging. Departments become unmanageable because everyone is using sickness as a way of forgetting their problems at the office.

Here's a neat solution: measure absences. This is how it's done:

■ Score days off sick either side of a weekend with 10 points.
■ Score days off sick either side of a bank holiday with 12 points.
■ Score single days off sick during the week, with 8 points.
■ Score linked mid-week days off sick with 2 points a day.
■ Score days off for long-term sickness with 1 point per week.

Use a period of not less than a month and not more than a quarter. This weighted method of scoring highlights the obvious skivers and does not penalise those who are genuinely ill.

Now add up the scores for each department and publish the results on the intranet, e-mail or notice board. Be sure everyone sees the results. Expect the following to happen:

■ Demonstrating that the issue has management attention will impact on the lead-swingers and reduce sickness absences immediately.
■ Departments with a high score will probably be the poor performers and will be impacting on other departments. Expect peer pressure to leverage down unacceptable and unwarranted absence levels.

Honestly, or your money back!

Cliques, circles and witches' covens

Organisations with poor morale are often infested by little groups who put themselves 'outside' the organisation, in the sense that they look to each other for mutual support and become semi-detached.

They sit, grumbling and festering and conspiring! Just what a paranoid manager needs… They are often the source of gossip. What they don't know, they make up.

✓ TIP

You can use gossip creatively. If you've got some good news to spread, whisper it, in confidence, to the company gossip. Stand back and wait for it to be spread!

There are two approaches. The first is to break the groups up, moving personnel to other parts of the organisation, changing working hours, or changing the work clique members so that they are disconnected from each other. That may not be a practical solution. It is disruptive and may exacerbate an existing morale problem.

The second solution is more Machiavellian. Try giving selected members of the group specific and special tasks for which they must report to you. Encourage them and praise them. Get them onside. In effect, create a positive clique around you. Exploit their talents, reward them with public praise and lift them out of their introspection.

16

Fault-finders and nit-pickers

There is absolutely nothing wrong with him that a miracle can't fix.

Alexander Woollcott

How do you deal with a fault-finder? Answer – don't have any faults! If only it were that easy. When staff take a pride in what they do, a grudging fault-finder rumbling away in the corner can be a real downer.

You really do have to nip their unwelcome interventions in the bud.

Fiona, I want you to remember the whole department has put a huge amount of effort into this. I think a lot of them feel your constant fault-finding is pretty hard to take. I want you to make a list of all the things that you see as wrong and go though it with me. Let's get the criticisms dealt with and out of the way.

You could try getting them to acknowledge what is good and help out, getting the rest out of the way:

Fred, I know this isn't perfect but we have managed to eliminate 90 per cent of the quality errors and guarantee claims. What do you think we should be doing to go the next step?

> **✓ TIP**
>
> Creative fault finders? Is there such a thing? Sure. Use them. They are often the masters of detail and they can be harnessed to use their talents more creatively:
>
> *I know you're very critical of this project, Christine, and you've found number of faults in it. I want you to have a good look at the programme before we submit it and point out anything else you think may not be right.*

If you have a nit-picker for a boss

To deal with generalised criticism of the 'This just won't do' variety, ask the boss to be specific. *'Boss, I hear your opinion that you're not happy with what I've done, but for me to put it right I need you to be more specific.'*

Invite criticism and try to stay clear of opinion. Focus on the specifics of what is wrong, and get the boss to see it in the context of the totality of the work. It can't be all bad, can it?

A sarcastic boss? Ugly. Sarcasm, the lowest form of wit? So they say. Don't treat it as wit. Don't laugh when the boss says of a colleague 'Look at her trying to be the customer relations department!'

In reply, say *'I think Mary does very well with the customers, she tries really hard to please them. Anyway, where would we all be without customers?'*

Nit-picking colleagues

Sitting next to fault-finders makes the working day seem longer. The trick is not to shun them or ignore them. The right approach is to get really close to them. Ask for their opinions as often as you can. When they start to moan and pick holes, ask them questions. Dig deep into their opinions, and demand they back up opinion with fact. I bet they won't have too many facts!

The more you dig, the less often they will find fault. Fault-finders often do their dirty work without much thought. It becomes a habit, a mindset and superficial. By questioning them, you make them think. That requires effort and they will soon pack it in.

On the positive side, by digging you might find the seeds of useful criticism that you can put to work, to improve what you are doing.

Staff who find fault, whine and grumble can be teased out of their mindset by getting them involved in solving the problem they are whinging about. 'The car park lighting is useless' deserves, *'Lucinda, I was thinking the same thing myself. I want you to look into the practicality and costs of upgrading it. Would you let me have some proposals by the end of next week?'* This approach occupies the fault-finder, shuts him or her up for a while, makes him or her feel important and gets the car park lights sorted!

✓ **TIP**

If you are a positive-minded soul, you will probably try to shut out the fault-finders of this world. Try another way: *'Karl, I really appreciate what you've said about this work. I've taken on board what you said and I think you've helped me to do a better job.'* See, now you've got a fan!

17

Gossip: a bush fire you can do without

There are many who dare not kill themselves, for
fear of what the neighbours might say.

Cyril Connolly

Gossip has to be one of the most corrosive influences on corporate culture. It has two sources.

The first is careless talk. Maybe some major change is in the offing. Perhaps something is going to impact on the organisation. People will be tense and uneasy. They will be looking for clues about their future. A careless word, a conversation overheard in a lift, the car park or the canteen, can start a hare running. This kind of thing happens. It is avoidable, and good management, timely communications and a commitment to openness can stop gossip dead in its tracks. That is a management issue, and there are management techniques to ensure that gossip is not given a chance.

The second type of gossip is probably the most damaging. It is the gossip that is started by people who don't have any facts. There are no fragments of information that they are trying to piece together. This is the sort of gossip that is started by the uninformed, the disenfranchised and the downright dim.

Was there ever a truer phrase than 'knowledge is power'? There are people in organisations who, in order to make themselves appear powerful, will create gossip and rumour. They want to make it look like they are 'in the know'. They can do the most enormous damage.

Of the few studies done around the organisational dynamics of gossip, one of the most telling was carried out by Anders Vidners, now a professor at Stockholm University but previously a corporate guru who worked with the Swedish pharmaceutical giant Astra (later to become the subject of a corporate merger and turn into Astra-Zeneca). Vidners showed that in large organisations one person could have a 'meaningful dialogue' with 15 other people during the course of an ordinary working day. Here's how gossip spreads; 15 × 15 × 15. Figure 17.1 makes it even clearer.

Spooky, isn't it? One person talking to 15 is bad enough. Fifteen talking to another 15 gets worrying: it means 225 people may have the wrong message. After that, the sums get silly: 225 × 15 = 3,375. Soon enough the whole world has got hold of the wrong end of the stick.

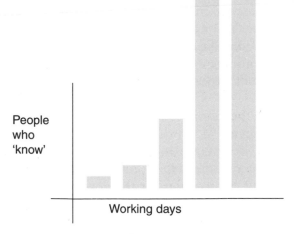

Figure 17.1 *Map of a bush fire – how gossip lights up your day!*

What started out as 'This month has a tight budget' becomes:

- ▣ This month we won't hit target.
- ▣ We've not been hitting target.
- ▣ We haven't hit target and the budget is being reviewed.
- ▣ They're reviewing the budget.
- ▣ There's going to be a review.
- ▣ There are going to be cuts.
- ▣ Cutbacks will mean job losses.
- ▣ There are bound to be redundancies.
- ▣ Hundreds of jobs will go.

The more the message is spread, the less accurate it gets. Gossip is like a bush fire. It starts as a spark and turns itself into a forest fire. It is almost impossible to stop and before you know it there's nothing left.

The answer to gossip problems

Rumour-mongers are immature, and the only real answer isn't always pleasant. You have to confront them. *'Harry, I need to ask you something. Did you say (repeat the rumour); is that right?'* Expect an answer along the lines of. 'Well it must be, because…'. Don't expect the culprit to own up. That's for the grown-ups!

Confronting the gossip is not enough by itself. You run the risk of them saying 'It must be true, they tried to shut me up.' The trick is to confront the gossip and put the record straight at the same time. *'Harry, what you are saying isn't true. The facts are…'*. So to confront the gossip, you need to have the facts.

Sometimes there will be sensitive issues that you can't deal with right away. In that case, try this:

Harry, what you are saying isn't true. There are very good reasons why, at the moment, it isn't possible to say anything about the issue, but we expect to be able to make a statement in the next 24 hours. My advice to you is to wait until you have all the facts before you say any more.

The next step is to be sure you make the statement on time. If you don't, you will be rewarded with more gossip!

✓ TIP

Need to get some information communicated through the organisation fast? Treat it like gossip!

Hazard warning

Don't think, for one moment, this is just a big company problem. Small organisations are just as prone to being burned by gossip. Small companies have customers, suppliers and associates. Gossip spreads inside and outside the organisation and can do some real damage to credibility and reputation.

Prevention is better than cure

Gossip can easily get out of hand and can be the devil's own job to eradicate. A good communications strategy is the answer. The sorts of issue that are likely to worry staff and get tongues wagging are easy to spot:

■ poor results;
■ the loss of a big order;
■ a potential take-over;

▓ a key member of staff leaving;
▓ a change of major supplier;
▓ moving premises.

Letting people know what is going on stops gossip dead in its tracks.

Corporate politics, sensitive negotiations, delicate issues can't always be brought into the public domain. Remember, because you can't speak doesn't mean others won't.

What's the answer? Easy: say you can't say anything:

> *I know there has been some rumour about (whatever the issue is). I'm anxious to put an end to the gossip. I can't say anything right now but I will be able to give some hard information on (name a sensible time-scale).*

Be sure you follow through on the promise, otherwise expect some more problems with gossip.

18

The customer is always right – really?

All English shop assistants are Miltonists. All
Miltonists firmly believe that 'they also serve
who only stand and wait'.

George Mikes

The customer is always right? Er, actually no. Well, I mean, yes.
If you see what I mean!

Customers can be a real pain: demanding, difficult and
downright belligerent. But they are also the clothes on your
back, the roof over your head and the shoes on your feet.

The world has moved on. There was a time when customers
would put up with second-best, accept excuses and be reluctant
to complain. Not any more. In this consumer driven, 24–7–365
economy, if you don't deliver, there is plenty of choice and
customers will move on. Sometimes customers will push to the
point where you have to make some serious decisions about
just how far you will and can afford to go. It's better to bring
the relationship to an end in a civilised way than have it ended,
for you, in a blazing row.

Customers don't always get it right. They complain when

they really have no right to complain, they exaggerate, lie and can be a crooked as a Great Train Robber. Laws protecting customers are abused and lawyers exploiting their no-win–no-fee new-found freedoms are probably another aggravation you can do without. Grim, isn't it? But the customer is always right!

✓ TIP

The real trick is not to have difficult customers! Deliver what and when you say you will, give value for money and be ready to act fast if something does go wrong, and you needn't read this section. If, on the other hand, you live in the real world, you might want to glance at it!

Dealing with difficult customers

No apologies for the over-use of the next word: communication. It is at the heart of good staff relations and it is at the heart of good customer/client relations. It is of course a two-way thing. To communicate, you've got to get the customer's attention and be sure you understand what they are asking for. Not sure the customer is paying attention, or they are unclear in what they want? Try this. *'I just want to make sure I've understood you correctly. To get this right, you will want...'* (Then describe what they are demanding.) This has the dual effect of clarifying the situation and, by playing back what they said, makes outrageous demands seem silly, even to those who made them!

Once clarified, translate it into an order, a specification or a record.

You want it when?

What about the really demanding customer? Offer less and do more, that's the key! Be sure not to get it the other way around. As always, it's in the words:

Oh, that's a tall order. You're setting us a real challenge here because we don't usually turn an order around in that time/make in that colour/get the paperwork through the system in that timescale/whatever, but we'll do our best.

By setting up the anticipation that you might not be able to deliver, when you do, you'll have one delighted customer. If you don't, you've created some room for manoeuvre.

✓ **TIP** Something gone really wrong? Go to visit the client. Even if you never normally visit, do it. Show the client he or she (or it) is worth the journey, the time and the cost. Look him or her in the eyes, read his/her body language and say 'We messed this up and I'm here to say sorry and to find out how we can put it right.'

Avoiding trouble

Get it in writing. Tedious? Yes, but a well-written contract has dug many folk out of a difficult situation. Don't think it has to be something like the Maastricht treaty. A simple note of who is going to do what, when and at what price is all that's needed.

Defining accountability and expectations is simple good practice. From time to time, everyone has a fallible memory. Later on, if there is a problem, you have the opportunity to say *'I've looked at the agreement we had and it seems pretty clear to me, you agreed we should (whatever the task or service was). I think you'll agree with me, that's exactly what we have done.'*

The really, really, really, really difficult customer

Try a chaperone. Appoint someone with special responsibility to look after a valued but difficult customer. Give the customer a reference point, easy access, a direct phone number and a named person. Sit back and watch the complaints fall. Many times complaints fester and get worse because they are not dealt with expeditiously, or the process of having a moan turns a disappointed customer into a difficult customer. Make it easy for someone to be difficult, and they won't be. Honestly – or your money back!

 ✓ TIP

How do they run their ship?

A really good guide to what prospective clients or customers might expect from you is how they run their business. If everything is lined up, shipshape, neat and tidy, that's your signal not to be sloppy. If they have a reputation for looking after their customers, delivering on time and offering terrific value, you know what you've got to do!

Remind them how good you are

Giving great value for money and stunning service? Tell your customers, remind them and then tell them again. How? Spell it out on an invoice. Step by step, itemise the components of what you are charging for. Avoid wording such as:

> To:
> Attend and repair Model Z134
>
> Total: £ 250 + VAT

Use the invoice as an advertisement. Try:

> To:
> Attend within 3 hrs of call out request + locate problem in Model Z134 using diagnostic equipment + carry out repair using replacement component from stock on service van + reassemble + clean and service generally + unit back in service within 45 minutes of attending.
>
> Total: £250 + VAT

I know which invoice I'd feel better about paying.

The screamer

Don't you just love a good scream? Babies do it all the time, just to get your attention. And we know it works. Screamers come in all shapes and sizes. They can be customers, colleagues, the boss, the neighbour or the teenage daughter. The solution is the same for all of them. Here's what you do:

Take a copy of this book and hit them on the head with it.

No, no, no! As much as you may want to do it, resist the temptation. First rule with a screamer is don't join in. Don't get into a decibel competition. Screamers are juvenile and wouldn't do it if they could see how silly they look.

Like all juveniles, they want attention, so give it to them. Listen, let them scream. Let the accusations, the smears, the insinuations, the abuse and rudeness fly over your head. Let them have a good blast. When they tire and stop for breath, pick your moment. Step in and say something.

The important thing here is to pick your moment. You won't silence a screamer, but you can wait until they run out of steam. So judge the moment and say *'Can we get to what's really wrong here? Help me understand...'* (go to the issues). It may not work the first time. Let the next instalment of invective pass you by and try again. Keep going, because it is the only way.

✓ TIP

One way to bring screamers down off the ceiling is to speak in a voice that is just a touch quieter than you would normally use. That way they have to shut up, pay attention and listen.

On the phone

No matter how bad it gets, never hang up. If you do, you have two problems to deal with: the whatever-it-was they were screaming about in the first place AND getting over the fact you slammed the phone down.

You can get off the line by saying *'I'm going to have to go now but I'll call you back in just two minutes.'* Don't do this to duck out of trouble – be sure to ring back. The chances are when you do ring back they will have calmed down. Well, that's the theory! It usually works – but no money back if it doesn't! Just stay calm.

> **✓ TIP**
>
> Never deal with a screamer, on the phone, sitting down. Stand up and the tone and texture of your voice will change. You can 'hear' body language. You'll sound more interested. Honestly!

In public

If the screamer is in public, you'll probably want to get him or her into a quieter, more private environment. Use the right words and some body language. Say *'OK, I think I understand, let's get to the bottom of it. Can we go to my office so that I can make some notes.'*

The next thing is the behaviour changer: the body language bit. Turn half away, gesture in the general direction of the office and take half a step but keep eye contact.

If you've judged it right, the screamer will follow you. If not, let him or her scream a bit longer and say the same again.

Hazard warning

Some people-management gurus will tell you to deal with a screamer by saying things like 'I'm not going to carry on with this if you shout at me' or 'Please don't use that language to me' or 'Please try to behave in a more mature fashion'.

The grim news is it will make the situation worse. There is no excuse for bad language and aggression, but highlighting it will simply ignite more trouble and invite another load of air.

Just stay cool and let it pass you by.

Screaming about service

A certain prime minister in a recent general election was made to look flat-footed by the relative of a patient who wanted to complain about the treatment the patient had had from one of the government's nice new hospitals.

'Not enough money, dirty wards, unacceptable waiting times.' The poor old PM mumbled about more cash for the health service and how his policies would take time and would the lady like to talk to him about it inside? Why should the dear lady 'go inside': she knew she had the world's press outside watching her!

The lesson here is to try to deal with difficult people in difficult situations on their own terms. What would have happened if the PM had said to her '*This is terrible, show me*', and then done the bit with the body language? It is a fair bet that she would have followed him and the ding-dong would have been conducted away from the gaze of the cameras.

If a member of your staff blows a gasket

He or she just loses it. Like a volcano, whoosh! If he or she is a member of staff you want to keep, life after a good scream will be difficult, but it can be managed.

Although you'll have to make it clear that 'that sort of behaviour' is not on, during the incident is not the time. Don't embarrass him or her. He or she will be embarrassed enough when it is over. Don't make it worse. Manoeuvre the person into a quiet place and say '*We need to sort this out. I'm going to leave you for a couple of minutes to collect your thoughts, then I'll come back and we'll go through it together.*'

Afterwards, insist that the individual apologises to anyone who was in earshot. It doesn't have to be a heavy, sackcloth and ashes apology. *'I think you do owe them an apology and to clear the air with them, don't you?'*

✓ TIP

Every once in a while even the best member of staff will have a funny five minutes and blow his or her stack.

The trick is to make the path back to normality as easy as possible. Avoid recriminations or referring to the incident once it has been dealt with. Move on.

When the screamer is the boss

Everyone ducks – that's what happens! The boss does have the power of the boot. Now is not the time to challenge him or her to use it. As with all screamers, the golden rule is to let them scream. It is the platinum, diamond-encrusted rule when the screamer is the boss. Ride out the storm, let it flow over you and under no circumstances scream back.

After the storm cometh the quiet. Pick your moment and say *'I know you are very cross but the whole incident was embarrassing for everyone. Can we please find some time to go through exactly what you want?'*

What's winding them up

Chances are, when anyone blows their stack, there'll be a hidden reason, not just work-related. Is it anything you can help with?

Dealing with very rude people without being very rude

Quite often, people are rude without knowing they are being rude. They are what workplace shrinks call overly focused.

They'll jump all over your conversations, interrupt, finish off your sentences and monopolise the discussion. Ever thought about why they do it? Quite often rudeness has its roots in shyness and a feeling of inadequacy.

The rude pig who jumps into your conversation probably doesn't look very shy, but inside him or her there is a little voice that says 'If I don't jump in, I'll never get my point across.' Seeing the rude pig in that context makes him or her more a person to feel sorry for than to get excited about.

The professional rude pig will monopolise a conversation and make it impossible for anyone else to get a word-in edgeways.

Let him or her ramble on. Sooner or later he or she will drift away from the subject in hand. Pick your moment, and break in with *'This is all very interesting but what has it got to do with the agenda item? Shouldn't we focus on...?'* Use that as a way of getting yourself and others back into the conversation. Don't think you'll be on your own. In a group meeting the others will recognise their time has come and support you.

✓ TIP

The classic, 24-carat, copper-bottomed, 100 per cent rude pig is verging on being a bully. Bullies need a victim, so don't be a victim.

Walk away politely and come back later. That will defuse the tension and send a signal that you will not put up with that!

Disguised rudeness

The classic example of this has to be the back-handed compliment, or the put-down.

You know the sort of thing: 'Good sales figures, Brian, but I guess they're not real sales. Most of them were from government procurement anxious to spend their budgets by the end of the financial year?'

Don't put up with it! Have some sense of self worth. *'Thanks, I worked hard on them. What do you mean by "not real sales"?'* Watch them back off.

19

Complaints: we love them

Six steps to success

Got a screamer? Ouch! Won't let you get a word in edgeways? Here's the fail-safe technique for dealing with a complaint:

- listen;
- sympathise;
- don't justify;
- make notes;
- agree a course of action;
- follow through.

Let's take it step by step.

Listen

Here's the trick: listen and let the other person know you are listening. Use body language and physical prompts to show you're listening.

- Make notes of what they are saying. Ask *'Do you mind if I make a note of what you are telling me?'*

■ Take the phone off the hook.
■ Ask your secretary to hold calls while you deal with an important matter.
■ Invite the person to come to your office. *'Would you mind if we move into my office? I want to make a full note of what you are telling me.'*

It costs nothing to listen, and the more attentive you are, the more you will diffuse the situation. Pay attention to what the complainant is saying, concentrate and ask questions: *'Just to clarify my understanding'*, or *'This sounds terrible, would you just tell me that bit again?'*

Sympathise

Sympathising is not the same as agreeing, it doesn't mean accepting liability and it doesn't signal that you have surrendered. What it does do is to help to take the heat out of the situation. A few well-chosen words reaffirm you are listening and you are not trying to duck out of the situation.

Here are a few well chosen words:

■ *I'm really sorry to hear what you're telling me.*
■ *That sounds awful to me.*
■ *That must have been very difficult for you.*

Don't justify

The irate person in front of you is not in the least bit interested in the fact that half the staff are off work with the flu, the delivery you were expecting hasn't showed, the boss is on your back for more sales, you crashed the car on the way to work, the youngest cried all night and you had a row with the other half.

It's not their problem. They won't want to know the fault is in manufacturing, someone else let you down, you've had an unexpected rush and the call centre is under three feet of water.

Whatever the reason, whatever the problem, now is not the time to bring it up.

There will be a time, later, to explain why things have apparently gone wrong. But in the life of the complaint, now is not the time. It is too early. At the right time, it is OK to say:

I'm not in any sense trying to justify what went wrong here, but you do need to know, we've had a fire in the warehouse and all our deliveries are behind. I know your delivery is urgent and I will go and see what I can do to bring it forward.

 Hazard warning

Don't say things like:

▓ I can't believe it.
▓ You're putting me on.
▓ This can't be true.
▓ You're joking.
▓ What? No, surely not!

Even if you don't believe it, there's no point in making a bad situation worse by calling a complainer a liar, or hinting you think they are. The objective here is to defuse the situation, deal with the complaint with the minimum collateral damage and get on with your life.

Make notes

There is something reassuring about having someone write down your complaint. This is not to say, write it down in the bureaucratic glory beloved of the old British Rail, or the forms at the dry-cleaners, when they've screwed up on your favourite outfit. That kind of administrative agony just brings the pains on.

What we are talking about here is making a simple record of who is complaining, when and what it's about. Why? First, it reinforces the listening message, and second, notes made contemporaneously might be a godsend if everything gets out of hand later on.

✓ TIP

A summary of the complaint, made at the time, is usually a reliable record of what happened and is made before the complainant has had time to embroider the problem or fester in the compost heap of compensation.

Agree a course of action

OK, what are you going to do next? You've listened, sympathised, made notes. What's next? Agree a course of action. How? Ask:

- How do you think we should take this forward?
- How would you like me to handle this from here?
- How do you see resolving the situation?

By asking these types of question you will get a feel for how far you will need to go to get this out of your in-tray. It doesn't mean you're capitulating or ready to roll over. It just gives you a sense of what it might take to resolve the issue.

Maybe what the complainant asks for is reasonable, within your responsibility to grant and you can deliver. In which case – job done.

On the other hand, it might be they are asking too much, it is outside your gift or the whole thing is starting to look like a put-up job. In this case a few more well-chosen words are called for:

- *'I know you will want me to get to the bottom of this, so I'm going to ask you to give me a couple of hours/days to look into this properly.'*

▪ *'I can't authorise what you are asking for, so I am going to take this matter to the manager and ask him(her) to help.'*

▪ *'There are several people involved in this matter and I am going to have to ask you to give me some time to sort it out.'*

▪ *'This seems very serious to me and I know you wouldn't want anyone else to have to go through it. I'll need time to make proper enquiries.'*

The next segment in handling a complaint is the pivotal bit. Without this, all the rest of the action has been a waste of time.

Follow through

In other words, deliver what you promised. If you agree to call someone back 'this afternoon, when I have made enquiries', be sure to do it. No news yet? No information to hand? No matter. Call back and say 'I know I promised I'd call you this afternoon, once I had made enquiries. Unfortunately, the person I need to speak to has been away from the building all day. He'll be back here tomorrow and I will speak to him and call you by lunchtime.' If there is still no news, do the same thing again. Keep doing it until you have a resolution.

Promise to mail a new part, extra thingamajig, or post a replacement widget? Do it, or call and say why you couldn't do it and agree another deadline. Follow-through is the most important stage in dealing with complaints.

So, what have we got? It sounds something like this:

Hazard warning

The easiest way to make a bad situation worse is failing to follow through. Telephone call, letter, e-mail: whatever it is, do it. Even if you can't deliver what you thought you could, call back and say so. Agree another deadline.

Mrs Bloggs, I need to listen to what you're saying properly. Can we move into my office so that I can make a note of what you are telling me?

Oh dear, this sounds like we have let you down/this is a big disappointment/you must be very upset with us.

Let me make a proper note of what you are telling me. Could you just tell me that bit again?

I'm not able to authorise what you are asking me to do. However, my supervisor/boss, the MD will be here this afternoon and I will ask her for her help. I'll call you back before the close of business.

Be sure you do call back.

Hazard warning

If you hear yourself sounding like this, read the previous few pages again:

I can't believe we got it this wrong. The problem is we've got three staff off with the flu and we're really behind in our order section. I'm not sure when I can sort this out. By the way, what did you say your name was?

✓ TIP

Once in a while, in every organisation, mistakes will occur. It is no great sin to get things wrong. It is a sin to get things wrong and not put them right, or to get things wrong too often, or, worst of all, to get things wrong and not know about it.

The trick is to learn from mistakes and near-misses. Organisations that encourage an openness about complaints, staff foul-ups and mistakes learn about their systems, protocols and approaches. Mistakes and complaints cost time and money, but they are also an opportunity. Handled correctly, a complaining customer can become an advocate and a champion.

Audit complaints, analyse them and use them as a stepping stone to better performance. Don't let them become a millstone.

e-difficult@yourplace

Having a laugh, innocent fun, office jokes. You must be used to them by now. Once the jokes were told around the tea trolley or in the canteen. Then it was the funny cartoons copied on the new Xerox machine. Now there is e-mail.

This is much more difficult to deal with. The office jokers have a new toy. More importantly, it is not just the office joker. It's the office jokers in all the other offices, far and wide, who can dump their stuff into your system.

Smutty jokes, lewd pictures, unacceptable stories whiz around the e-mail systems and get circulated indiscriminately. Litigation, writs and battles are just an e-mail away. The problems will start internally, then the outside world will come crashing down on the heads of unsuspecting management.

Unless you get a grip on the office jokers, racists and the smutty minded, expect problems. Difficult lawsuits alleging everything from sexual discrimination to breach of confidence have been sparked by companies without proper e-mail policies and planning.

E-mail policies are fundamental to the way good organisations run their affairs.

Hazard warning

E-mails can easily be faked or fiddled with and printed-out messages can be similarly counterfeited. In some systems, planting a blank e-mail into a file history makes it possible at a later stage to go back and fill it in with any message you like. This is a trick likely to fool everyone, even an experienced observer.

A storage system that is tamper-proof does not come cheap and will eat up a storage disc faster than an American termite can chomp its way through a house.

If you've found someone circulating bad taste e-mails, try this:

Fred, I know you think this kind of thing is funny, and to some people perhaps it is. But there are some others who will be offended, and I cannot risk the company, its reputation and the chance of a law suit or tribunal. I'm telling you it has to stop, and if it happens again there will be a formal warning and you risk disciplinary action.

Here are six ideas to avoid e-fail with e-mail:

Check ✔

- ▓ Warn all staff with an 'on-screen' message about the organisation's rules for e-mail. Use the screen saver to do it at zero cost.
- ▓ Make it clear that e-mail is not confidential and will be routinely monitored. More importantly, hammer home the fact that e-mail is not a substitute for the kind of conversation that used to take place in the canteen, lavatory or lift.
- ▓ Stamp out digital gossip; bar the transmission of personal mail, jokes, smutty material and non-business messages. American experience shows staff who are offended can sue their employer.

Someone is bound to try a case here, sooner or later.

■ Set up in-house e-training to help staff understand the rules. This might persuade a court that you have taken your responsibilities seriously. Incorporate e-mail policies into contracts of employment.

■ Install one of the new programmes to monitor e-mail for key words and phrases, to flag up offensive material.

■ Decide on archive policies now: what to keep, how long to keep it, how to keep it and who is responsible. Cost electronic archive processes and budget for it – the outlay is more than you think. Disc and tape space doesn't come cheap, but it's not as expensive as a few days at the high court.

21

Meetings, bloody meetings!

It always strikes me as strange that people become so difficult over the topic of meetings. People are disruptive in meetings, dismissive of meetings and destroy the creative energy that can come from a really good meeting.

As I travel around talking with groups of managers and bosses, high on the list of 'moans' is the escalating amount of time spent in meetings.

My answer? Tough, you'd better get used to it! Meetings are not an add-on, not an interruption of the working day, and not an appendage. Meetings are management.

Meetings are the inevitable consequence of shaping products and services around the needs of customers, clients and the people who provide the cash to pay our wages. Collaborating, merging, strategic alliances, developing products, interdepartmental liaison all mean more meetings.

Planning meetings, brainstorming, progress meetings, outcome meetings, case conferences. Policy making, negotiating, settling disputes, trust building, managing change. Meetings about meetings!

What's the answer?

Get tough and get into technology

Do you know how much your meetings cost? That's the first step in getting tough.

Think about this

In a recent BT business survey, it was estimated that most European companies spend more on business travel than they do on advertising.

Here's my eight-step, Genghis Khan guide to making meetings work.

1. Work out how much it costs to hold a meeting. Time is as valuable as any other organisational asset. Calculate the cost per hour of holding a meeting, write it in big letters and pin it to the wall. Don't be embarrassed, just do it! Hammer home the cost of dealing with difficult people who dither, are indecisive, spend time on gossiping and tittle-tattle.

2. How many times have you been to a meeting and it's obvious someone hasn't read the agenda or done their homework? Make sure you never attend a meeting unprepared. Make it clear you've done your homework and don't have any truck with people who haven't. Don't be afraid to say *'We are all busy people and I think we owe it to each other to do our homework – don't you?'* Then fix the miscreant with your most winning smile. Bet they never turn up unprepared again!

3. Always insist that meetings start on time. Speak up, say: *'I think everyone knows we should get started at 3 pm and*

unless we do I'm concerned that some of us will overrun into our next commitments.' Be firm. Start on time: late-comers will soon get the hang of it. If they complain, smile and say *'I'm sorry but the start time is on the agenda and we all have other things to move onto'*, or *'We couldn't really wait around for you as we've not heard from your office that you would be late. We didn't know if you're were delayed or not coming.'* And smile the dazzling smile only you can do!

4. Agenda – make sure there is one. No agenda? Don't waste your time. Meetings without agendas are like a journey into a jungle with no map. If the agenda is not set in advance, ask the chair person *'Before we start, shall we make a list of the items we need to cover?'* If you're really pressed for time, think about asking for the agenda items that involve you to be taken together and when you're through, push off! Try to avoid 'any other business'. It's a gossip's charter. Do that in the car park, or over a cuppa before you start.

5. Always make sure the meeting runs to time. If you're in charge, make sure there is a big, conspicuous clock that everyone can see. Announce what time you intend to finish and keep an eye on the clock. It may mean cutting items short. Say *'I'm looking at the clock and if we are to do justice to the rest of the agenda I think we are going to have to reach a conclusion on this item.'* If you are not in charge, be obvious in taking off your wristwatch, put it on the table and keep it in your eyeline. Don't be afraid to say to whoever is running the meting, *'I've got an eye on the time and I'm concerned that if we don't move on, we'll have items that we will not be able to do justice to.'*

6. Dopey chairperson? This is grim news. Try having a quiet word. Express your concerns about running to time or wasting time on gossip and chit-chat. If all else fails, grab the initiative and chair the meeting from the floor. Try

phrases such as *'Do you think we should move on?'* or *'This is interesting but I think we should try and stick to the agenda, don't you?'* Don't forget the smile!

7. If there is a tricky or complex item to be discussed, don't wait for the meeting, get on the phone in advance and lobby for support. Take time to explain the detail and ask for backing. It speeds up the meeting and works a treat.

8. Do you really need to have a meeting? I mean really, really, really need to have one? Try to get a delegated authority from your group to deal with some issues with colleagues over the phone, or through e-mail.

Technology

Once-glamorous options such as video-conferencing have now become routine. PCs with video cameras are cheap and can be linked internally using the network facility that comes with most Windows platforms after version 95.

However, do you really need pictures? Try conference telephone calls. Internally, most phone systems have the capability. The only problem is, no one knows how to set it up! Make the IT department earn its keep – find out!

Think it might be too expensive? Look at the piece of paper you've pinned to the wall. How much an hour does a meeting cost you?

Meetings can be boring, dull, uninspiring, flat, slow, heavy, languid, fun, happy, a laugh, productive and just about everything in between. Don't overlook the role that the meeting environment can play.

To meet or not to meet

That is the question. Here is the answer!

Difficult people become more difficult when a meeting content is poor or there is no obvious reason for them to have been dragged halfway across the territory for something that could have been achieved on the telephone.

Think of a meeting as nothing more than a management tool. Just like e-mail, fax, memos, phone calls and handwritten notes, meetings have a role to play. They are not the first line of defence or a knee-jerk reaction to a problem. Of all the communications mediums available, a meeting will be the most costly. Use meetings wisely.

To meet or not to meet: your call.

have a meeting if:	don't waste everyone's time if:
You're the boss/leader/manager and there is an issue that you need advice or guidance to deal with.	There is insufficient known about the problem, no data or information.
There is a problem to solve or a decision to make and you want to involve a group in getting a grip on it, especially if you need buy-in to implement a solution.	The same result can be achieved by phone, e-mail or memo.
Maybe no decision is needed but there is something that needs to be clarified, face to face.	The meeting would deal with a burning issue, tempers are running high and there is a risk of a row. Use time to cool the group down and allow them to become more objective.

You have a concern about an issue that you want to share with your group.	The subject matter is highly confidential and a leak would be a disaster. Remember, there is no such thing as a secret.
There is a cross-functional problem that needs to be addressed by a range of people .	The topic is trivial.
There is confusion over lines of responsibility.	You've already made up your mind about what to do. Don't turn your group into a difficult bunch by treating them as a rubber stamp.
The group have indicated that they want to meet.	At stake are personal issues such as letting staff go, remuneration and individual performance. In the main, all that's best done one-to-one.

 Hazard warning

Beware of 'regular meetings'. They invite routine, and routine is the death of inspiration.

Think about this

The real trick in dealing with difficult people at meetings is not to give them the opportunity to become difficult. Sounds obvious? That's because it is. Most good management is founded on common sense. If you know an item is causing problems for someone, talk to that person in private, before the meeting. Encourage the quiet ones by telling them that you'll be asking them for their input on a certain item. Quieten the boisterous ones (without discouraging them) by asking them to hold back:

I know you are an expert on this topic, Ivan, but could you hold back and let some of the members of the group have time to talk about this in non-technical terms, then I'll ask for your view. Thank you.

You'll avoid difficult people at meetings if you get organised in advance. Here are 20 basic steps that should avoid some little local difficulties.

Done it

Doing it

1. Plan the who, what, where, when and why.
2. Be sure there is an agenda and it reaches people in good time.
3. Think about times and access.
4. Get the meeting venue environment right. Arrive in plenty of time and spend time, making sure it is set out in the way that you want.

5. Start on time and let the latecomers catch up. (Only delay the start of a meet-ing if there is a well-recognised travel problem, and even then by no more that 20 minutes. Otherwise you'll never catch up the time. Better to cancel and set an new date if there is real travel grief.)

6. Make sure everyone knows who everyone is. Get them to introduce themselves.

7. Make sure everyone knows why they are there, and what role they are playing.

8. Stick to the agenda. If you have to revise it (owing to lack of information, or because some key player has failed to turn up) do it at the start.

9. Use time as an ally. Set time limits for discus-sion. Don't allow one item to eat up all the time and leave the rest of the agenda stranded.

10. Pick up on action items or to-do updates from previous meetings.

11. Focus on the agenda items. Don't allow wavering, scandal (however juicy) or tittle-tattle to deflect you.

12. Keep an eye on who is speaking and who is quiet. Distribute the time and opportunity for contributions.

13. Keep minutes/notes and be clear who is to follow up, doing what, by when.

14. Check to make sure everyone under-stands.

15. Set the time and date of any subsequent meet-ings and, if possible, develop the draft agenda.

16. Don't have 'any other business' – it's a gossip's charter.

17. If you've not paid for the venue, leave it as you found it.
18. Prepare and circulate minutes.
19. Plan and follow through follow-ups.
20. Evaluate the meeting, your handling of it, and ask for feedback.

Meetings-r-us

Here are a few of the characters you're likely to come across sitting around the table, and here are some suggestions on how to read them and deal with them.

Dinosaurs

Dinosaurs are unwilling or unable to move on, accept a new idea or new working practices. They make 'black and white', 'right and wrong' statements, and display clear prejudices and rigid opinions. They are uncomfortable with abstract or new thinking.

How to deal with them

Remember the first rule of change management: respect the past and take the best of it into the future. Move to a discursive approach. Agree with them, disagree with part of what they say, deflect criticism and reflect together on what comes next. *'David, look at it from the company's point of view. We cannot stand still. Over time, everything changes and we must move on. We need to think about efficiency and profitability so that we can survive and we all still have a job.'* Or *'With respect, David, don't you think it is time to let this go and move on?'* You can appoint them as guardians of the past. Make them archivists, custodians. Be active in handling history: *'David, we've got to use this new approach but I'm anxious not to throw the baby out with the bath-water. What are the three most important things we take with us into this new approach?'*

Doodlers

Doodlers make more or less elaborate drawings on notepaper while you are talking.

How to deal with them
Does it matter? Are you just cross with yourself that you can't get their undivided attention? If they appear to be on the ball and keeping up, ignore it.

If you think it is a symptom that they are not paying attention, use their names occasionally, ask them to write notes of the meeting, if you are using a flip chart, let them make the record. If you want to be the American meetings guru, recognise a doodler's artistic talents and get him or her to product a visual representation of the decisions and action items from the meeting.

Eager puppies

Eager puppies keep trying to help, but their interventions do more harm than good.

How to deal with them
Use body language, nods and smiles, but don't initiate verbal interaction. Standing or sitting, incline your body away from the section of the room in which they are sitting. This sends a strong non-verbal signal that you're not paying attention. If they miss the point, don't be tempted to score points or embarrass them. You need to keep them engaged. Just remake the point and explain again what you meant. Or ask them to explain the relevance of their remark: *'I'm not sure how that fits in, Suzanne?'* With any luck, saying it twice will make it

seem stupid – even to Suzanne! The rest of the meeting participants will recognise what's going on and give you loads of
Brownie-points for patience.

Deflect their misplaced enthusiasm by brining others in:
'Suzanne, what do you think about Mary's point?' A quiet
word in the coffee break might make life easier for the second
half: *'Suzanne, I know you're an enthusiast for this, but to help
me get the others more involved, would you mind holding-off
during the next session?'*

Exhibitionists

Exhibitionists ask embarrassing questions about their personal
situation or indulge in extreme self-revelation, wash dirty linen
in public or launch into self-focusing anecdotes. This in turn
embarrasses others with their candour.

How to deal with them

Move on a swiftly as you can. *'Thank you for that, John. Now
lets think about what we have to do next.'* Try to refocus the
group: ask *'How do you think this personal experience fits in
with what we're discussing?'* Be firm. Point out sincerely and
straightforwardly that they are out of order, flash them your
winning smile and move on. The others will support you.
People hate to be embarrassed – even in groups.

Experts

Experts want to be recognised as expert. They want the spotlight on them and are determined they know as much as you, if
not more! They interrupt to disagree with facts, tell stories and
creates opportunities to demonstrate their own expertise.

How to deal with them

Thank them for their contributions, reassure them that
their knowledge is valuable. Give them specific tasks and

deliverables. Ask them for specifics or details that reinforce your message. Treat them as co-leaders, ask them for help on a really difficult problem and consult with them during the breaks. Experts are often insecure and need to demonstrate they know their stuff. Let them do it and use them as a resource. If they get really intrusive, bog them down in detail and work!

Gripe-masters

Gripe-masters are fatalistically negative in everything, including their body language. They shrug their shoulders, sigh and complain about everything. 'I didn't want to come in the first place.' They moan and whinge if asked to do anything or make a contribution.

How to deal with them

Reflect what they've been saying by repeating it back to them, and ask for other people's views. *'So you're saying, Gloria, there's no way this can ever work.'* (Wait for the response.) *'Do we all agree with that?'* Ask them to consider the consequences of their views. *'Gloria, if we all thought like that, where would the team end up?'* If they are intellectually up to it, ask them to be devil's advocates and put the other side of the argument. Discuss their reservations and negativity out of the meeting. Give them a chance to address the meeting and get their moans off their chests. Give them an airing and them move on. Draw a line: *'Gloria, I think we've given your position a good airing. Now I think most of us agree it is time to move on – isn't that right, everyone?'*

Hijackers

Hijackers want to take over the meeting. They do things like suggesting time could be more usefully spent on another topic, ask questions that lead you away from the topic, and try to use the meeting to resolve a problem personal to them.

How to deal with them
Refocus the meeting by thanking them for their observations and remind them of the topic under discussion. *'Hillary, if I understand you correctly, you are talking about... We are really focusing on...'* Then ask the group in which direction they want to go. They will support you – or your money back! Ask for their help to change the meeting structure to better address the needs of all participants. Keep checking with the group it's what they want! It usually isn't.

Hostile people

Hostile people interpret every new idea as a personal attack on their behaviour or knowledge. They question everything, challenge usefulness and relevance, refuse to play a part.

How to deal with them
Name them, use them as an example: *'Let's imagine that Harry's team have started using the new system and has a problem with...'* This draws them into the centre of events. If you know they are likely to be hostile, think ahead. *'Today we need to share our experiences... We've obviously done this similarly before... If there's anyone who doesn't think they can help their colleagues and doesn't want to join in, now is the time.'* This gets buy-in and it is hard for Harry to backtrack.

Above all, be sensitive as to why they are hostile: jealousy, left behind, passed-over for promotion – there'll be a reason.

Jokers

Jokers can't stop telling jokes and funny stories. They make fun of serious topics, make (vulgar) innuendoes, never miss a pun, and mock others in the meeting.

How to deal with them

If it is tolerable, try and build on it. Don't stifle it, use it. Not responding to humour can make a good leader look like a miserable stick in the mud. However, there is a line to draw. The smut you can always do without, especially in a male-dominated environment with few women co-workers. Some women have learned to put up with this sort of thing, but why should they? *'Jason, we all like to laugh, but I think we can leave that kind of story for the pub, don't you?'* Fix Jason in the eye and give one of your award-winning smiles: *'This is important stuff, now let's get through it.'* Don't be afraid to confront Jason: *'I'm sorry but that sort of story is OK for social occasions where people can choose to be. At work we have to respect each other, so cut it out.'* Try non-verbal shut-ups. Ignore what they say and shift your posture to avoid any eye contact. After inappropriate interventions choose a serious point and ask Jason to make a joke out of it. Ask for Jason's help in a project where his humour can be a positive force.

Nit-pickers

Nit-pickers want to follow rules, even to the detriment of efficiency. They interrupt to quibble with details, point out spelling missstaykes during slide presentations. They exasperate others with long-winded analyses and explanations.

How to deal with them

Use the technique of self-revelation. *'Natalie, thank you for pointing that out. Spelling is not my strongest point – look out for the next one!'* Use anecdotes or metaphors to tell a story in which there is a need for flexibility. Thank them for reminding everyone of the rules and explain why there is a need to do something different on this occasion. Explain, *'Natalie, that is not the level of detail I really want to get into today. I know it is important but if we don't move on we'll run out of time.'*

Rivals

Rivals are two people who use the meeting to 'get at each other', needle each other and score points. One tries to make the other look a fool. They make humorous, sarcastic or even aggressive put-downs of each other and use the topic as ammunition against one another.

How to deal with them

No messing here; ask them to keep it for outside the meeting. *'Greg, Tim, whatever is going on between you two, keep it till after the meeting. I'm not here to referee a private row, we're all here to get some work done.'* Try being reflective: *'If I understand you two (three, four, more? Help!)... you want to use this meeting to sort out your difficulties. How does the rest of the group feel about this? Do we want to watch the end of this, or finish the meeting?'* The rest will stick with you – or your money back! Refocus them, give them tasks to do. Institutionalise their rivalry: *'We know you two are not having a personal go at each other. You come from two different departments who work differently and handle quite different parts of the process. However, for the purposes of getting through this meeting, can I ask you two to think of yourselves as working together as part of this group?'*

Show-offs

Show-offs seek the spotlight to prove themselves. They are not interested in helping you, only in impressing others. They put you down to score points, monopolise discussions and in the process alienate others. The sort my mum calls a big head!

how to deal with them

Usually this type is deeply insecure. People who are really good at something aren't worried about anyone else. Take them on. Ask for specifics. Give them some rope and the chances are some other member of the group will censure them. Give them a task to do, so they can shine. Ask them for some help with a project. Use their energy to your advantage. If all else fails, *'Sidney, I know you're very conversant with all this, but the rest of the group don't have the same expertise. I want them to get a feel of the issues, at their own pace – which is what I expect you had to do, in the beginning. I'm going to ask you to hold off in the meetings to let the others get up to speed. Otherwise they'll just sit and watch you and me have a conversation. Not good, is it?'*

Shy people

Shy people avoid eye contact, blush easily, and speak rarely and in a quiet voice. They never volunteer information. (It's not just the girls who blush – boys do it too.)

How to deal with them

If they make a rare contribution, build on it, even if it is not the best comment you've ever heard on the topic. Praise prises open the shy ones: *'Simon, that's a very good point. What do you think about...?'* Follow it up as soon as you can with a closed question. Use their name in any example you give. Deal with the odd shy one by pretending the whole group is bashful: *'I understand there are some of you who are here for the first time and may be shy and don't like to speak in front of colleagues. OK, no doubt several others will compensate by giving their opinions loud and clear. The important thing is that before we finish the meeting everyone will have made their point. You are all here because we know you have something special to contribute, and I we want to hear it.'* Ask for opinions – but from a professional, not personal, point of view. *'So, Sylvia, what is the nursing perspective on this?' Or, 'Ian, what does the IT department make of this?'*

Sleepers

Sleepers yawn, stifle bigger yawns, their eyelids droop, they close their eyes and they are on the way out!

How to deal with them

Try and reinvigorate them; use their name, ask a question. Have a break, open a window. Be sympathetic. They probably had an early start, travelled miles and were up all night with the baby. Give them non-verbal permission to have kip! Anyway, after lunch be sure to say *'Anyone over 50 has my permission to have a nap, while the rest of us get on with this and make the decisions.'* That's guaranteed to keep them awake!

Slow coaches

Slow coaches keep getting it wrong, consistently volunteer remarks and ask questions that show they haven't understood, and answer questions incorrectly.

How to deal with them

Avoid embarrassing them, otherwise you will snuff out any enthusiasm and lose their contribution. Reframe your question or remarks. Take the blame: *'Christopher, I don't think I made myself very clear, what I was trying to say was....'* Or, *'No, Christopher, let me just stop you there. I didn't explain that very well.'* Use a recapping technique. Ask the question and whatever the response, restate the position: *'Does anyone else feel we need to recap this point? Well, in case there is and you're too shy, let me just quickly go over it again.'*

Speedy Gonzales

Speedy Gonzales is always one step ahead when asking questions, and is impatient with slower colleagues. He or she asks to move on before you are ready, and finishes exercises and assignments well before others.

How to deal with them

Ask for patience, explain why others need more time. *'Gonzales, you're a real whiz at this but the others are not as familiar and need more time. Let's not spoil it for them. I know you'll know the answers but can I ask you to hold off and give the others a chance to answer and become as confident as you are?'* If they are really good, give them stuff to do: the more complicated the better!

The sneaky ones

Sneaky people seem to be waiting to trap you. They jump in to demonstrate that you are prejudiced or unprofessional. They point out inconsistencies in arguments.

How to deal with them

Remember the second rule of dealing with difficult people. If they trap you, use your winning smile, apologise and thank them for identifying the problem. Ask them to be the watchdog, ask for a critique or views when none are forthcoming. Put pressure on them to find a fault and invite them to give feedback. They'll soon calm down. Honestly – or your money back!

Trouble makers

Trouble makers want attention – even if it's negative. They make remarks that are aggressive or insulting, and ask questions rudely. They express negative attitudes with hostility to you, the meeting or others. They may disagree loudly and offensively.

How to deal with them
Repeat what they say back to them and the group. '*Tom, if I understand you right, what you're saying is...*' Turn to the group. '*Is that how you would put it?*' The answer will be no. The trouble maker will realise he or she is making trouble for him- or herself by making enemies with the group.

Whisperers

These types make whispered comments to their neighbours.

How to deal with them
Remember, there is only one whisperer – the others are whisperees! They are often the unwilling victims of a whisperer. If they are, make an excuse for them to move to another place in the room: less draughty, less sunny, nearer the radiator, nearer the door as they may have to leave early. Otherwise refocus the whisperer's attention by naming them, asking a question. Make eye contact so they know you are aware of their whispering and then use body language to cut them off.

Woolly thinkers

Woolly thinkers make vague abstract contributions, and ask rambling unclear questions.

How to deal with them
Say: '*Willie, I'm sorry but I'm not sure I understood your point. You feel that...?* Tail off and let them make the point again. Clarify contributions with who, what, when, where, how,

specifically. Appeal to the rest of the group: '*Am I being dim? I didn't really get the point Willie is making. Can anyone help me out here?*' The group will come to your aid (promise, or your money back!) and probably, in the process, have a go at Willie to smarten up his act!

The five golden rules that make meetings productive

Don't start with a blank piece of paper

You've heard the expression 'Let's start with a blank piece of paper.' Don't bother, it doesn't work. It is easier for people to agree amendments, shuffle priorities and develop a process. Get something down on paper and be prepared for it to be trashed. No matter, it will focus people. Open with:

> *This is the first time we've tried to solve this/plan something like this/deal with this issue, In the spirit of getting the juices flowing I've made some notes/suggestions/ideas/milestone points. They are not written in stone, so feel free to trash them, but let's use them to get us started.*

Technicians and experts can be difficult to focus

It's easy to get bogged down in the detail. Experts and technicians can engage everyone with calculations that will tell us how many angels can dance on the head of a pin. Go for the 80 per cent rule. If you can get agreement on 80 per cent of the deal/project/idea, then go for it. The rest will evolve. Use timings, objectives and outcomes as your allies, and benchmarks to make sure the propellerheads and anoraks deliver their tangled-up bits.

Ask them if they have the power to say yes

If you're meeting, negotiating with or planning a partnership deal, make sure the others not only have the power to say 'yes', but have a budget they can authorise or can give a binding signature on a piece of paper. If in doubt, don't waste your time – ask. Do they have the power to buy in? Say *'My company authorises me to spend up to £5 million on this sort of project/sign off this type of deal/commit the company without referring back. Are we all in the same position?'*

Spell out the objectives and ram home the process

Meetings can easily become out of focus. Be clear at the outset what the objectives are, and take time to explain how the processes work. Be sure everyone understands the 'map' and get on with the job. If anyone starts to wander, remind them of what you are all trying to achieve. It is also important for everyone to know the key deliverables and the timeline. Spell it out, and if your neck is on the block if the project fails, keep in touch with everyone (outside the meeting cycle) to make sure they are on target to deliver.

Make sure you have minutes or a record

Never have a serious meeting without making notes or keeping minutes. Circulate them in good time, before the next meeting and as soon as possible after the meeting took place. Invite comments and corrections before the next meeting – this is to make sure things are sorted out whilst memories are still fresh. If you are running the meeting, it's not always a good idea to have to make the notes as well. Get someone to do them for you. It's a good job to give to a knit-picker or a show-off: keeps them occupied and feeling important!

22

If things don't change they'll stay the same

There are four Cs in change

Do you remember the early 90s management buzz-phrase, change management? I've never really understood the meaning of that expression. What is the purpose of management if it is not to see through change? Change is at the very heart of management. If things didn't change, we could get by with a whole lot of administrators and bureaucrats. They're cheaper to employ.

Indeed, some of the managers I come across are little more than process managers. The test of real managers is their ability to manage change. It takes leadership, courage and an understanding of what makes people tick.

Why do people hate change? Here are the answers. There are four Cs in change:

- cross;
- confused;

■ cast-off;
■ chaos.

Cross that things are changing? You bet! That will give way to being confused about what is happening. Confusion will give way to a feeling of being left behind or being unwanted. The result is chaos, in the sense that disaffected people will look for another job, good people will jump ship (while they know they can) and the rest will work in a battlefield of smouldering resentment that makes it impossible to see what's happening.

 Hazard warning

The four Cs are not phases we all go through, and the passage from one to the other is not necessarily a pathway that everyone will follow. But you can bet that all of us will go through some of them and some of us will go through all of them.

Understanding the four Cs in change is at the heart of what you need to know about managing change. They are the fundamentals.

They are the emotional responses through which people will go. The workplace has changed a great deal and no one expects a job for live. We all work where we work for a variety of reasons. The reasons span from 'the only place I can get a job', through to 'I love the work and the people I work with'. They can be 'I'm using this job as a stepping stone to a better job', right across the spectrum to 'I'm marking time till I retire.'

You could list a thousand different reasons why a thousand different people work where they do. What do they have in common? With very rare exceptions, people all work because they have to. They need the money. In other words, they need the security. Change threatens security. It's as simple as that. If working people don't feel secure, they worry, they become difficult and their performance drops.

Dealing with difficult people through a period of change

The first thing is to expect people to be difficult! Even the ones who are usually a delight to work with – expect the worse! Remember, it's the security thing. Security (or the lack of it) eats into the nice people along with the not-so-nice people.

> **✓ TIP**
>
> It is seldom the case that everything has to be changed. The trick of the great change-masters is to recognise the past and take the best of it into the future.

Cross

Cross? Of course, wouldn't you be? You've been a loyal employee in a job for ages. You've done your best and given everything that has been asked of you. Suddenly someone wants to change everything around. You'll go home and moan to your family, you'll moan to your friends and you'll moan to the people you work with.

What's the answer? Easy. Ask '*Christopher, I know you're cross about the changes that are taking place. Tell my why and let's see if there is anything we can do*': a few simple words designed to get the conversation focused. Expect 'Don't ask me. No one ever listens to me.' Come back with '*I'm sorry you feel that way. I'm listening now. What do you think I should know?*' Ask people what was good about their job before the change.

Don't raise expectations and do be realistic. However, you can be sympathetic and you can be understanding and supportive. *'I know change is difficult for us all, but if we don't move to a more up-to-date working practice, our overheads will continue to rise and that affects our competitiveness.'* Or *'I know how much you've put into your work and that is the reason we'd like you to try doing it another way. Who better to give it a real try for a couple of months and be able to evaluate it against some solid experience?'* Agree a course of action that involves poor old Christopher 'cross'.

Confused

If you've been doing the same job for years, probably in the same way, you'll be confused when some grey suit comes along and changes everything. It's more than the 'job-thing'. This time it is more about self-image and a feeling of loss. This is a common feeling among employees who have been with the organisation for a long time. Change can give them a genuine feeling of loss.

They will be wondering how (or even if) they fit in. Highlight the changes and how they can lead to a lot more job satisfaction. Say *'Colin, you've done a great job for us and we hope that the changes will make the job easier/faster/quieter/safer/more satisfying/give you more [less] customer contact.'* Concentrate on the positive side of the changes and how they translate into a benefit for confused Colin.

Cast-off

Of all of the four Cs, this one has to be the most common. There is another C lurking behind this: communication, that 13-lettered word again, unlucky for some. The bigger the company, the more complex the change, the faster it is introduced, the more people will not have a clue what is going on.

This one needs all of your patience. You may well have sent out 27 tonnes of inter-company newsletters, held goodness knows how many briefing sessions and bombarded the organisation with helpful e-mails. There will still be one or two (or more often more) individuals who still don't know what's going on.

Listen to people's views on their new department, or workplace, or job. You'll here them say 'There's no place for an older person like me any more.' Explain how they fit into the new organisation, the reasons for change and the part they can play:

> Catherine, I'm sorry if all this change has made you feel we don't value you. That is really not the case. The important thing is the new company needs to have experienced people like you around, we need your know-how to help us develop into the future. Now, tell me, what are you not sure about?

Now here's the trick. Don't leave it there. People who claim to be confused and to not know what is going on sometimes use it as a defence mechanism. In other words, they don't want to know what is going on. So agree some objectives that are related to the change and monitor the outcomes. That way the 'confused' become engaged.

Give Catherine the 'confused' a place to hide and often she will!

 Hazard warning

Small companies have communication gaps, too. Bosses often think that because it is a small company everyone knows what's going on – not true. Small companies have to communicate too!

✓ TIP

Two tricks in managing change: spell it out, and interest people. Spell out the changes as often and as clearly as you can. Be prepared to clarify again and again.

Second, do it in a way that interests people. Explain the changes, not from the corporate point of view (that needs to be done, but not now), but from how it will affect the individual, what it means to them, personally, day to day. This engages people in the change process on a personal level.

Chaotic

'I have no idea where I fit into this mess. I don't know what I'm supposed to be doing. All I know is, this is a mess.' You're bound to hear that sometime from someone.

Start with a confidence builder. Ask Charlie to spell out what he thinks the changes are, then say *'Well, that's a pretty good summary. Let's take a moment and look at the detail.'* No matter what he's said, it's time to start at the beginning and get Charlie the Chaotic back on track. It's better than saying, *'Charlie, even a complete idiot could understand this. What's up with you?'*

Hazard warning

When does management become manipulation? The really great managers maintain the self-confidence and balance of those around them. They encourage staff to believe in themselves, and find ways of showing staff they believe in them.

23

Dealing with conflict: 10 steps to cooling it

Deadlines, targets, goals, objectives, measurement, governance, pressure and burdens of responsibility. Is it any wonder working relationships collapse under the strain? Tensions, anxiety, stress, unease all mount up. Somehow the fuse gets lit and...

Bang!

Well what did you expect?

What can you do about it? Is conflict inevitable? No, it is not. Here are 10 simple steps to take to defuse the situation, take the sting out of the issue. You can be the one who takes it all in his or her stride, and you can be the one to be cool under fire. You can be the peace maker and you don't have to be the living incarnation of Mother Teresa to do it. It's simple, really.

■ Manage aggression face to face. Not by e-mail, fax, memo, voicemail, notes or answering machine. Peace makers 'do it face to face'. Difficult? Sometimes, yes it is. But leaving messages and sending billets-doux just creates a compost in which resentment, grudges, rancour, spite and hostility will grow.

■ Demonstrate you understand. Use the phrase 'I understand', but use it with care. Saying, 'I understand' can appear supportive and knowing. It also invites the response, 'What do you mean, "you understand"? How could you possibly know?' Better to use the concept of understanding, but in a different way. Try *'I can see you're very upset. Sometime ago I had a big bust-up with someone and was furious and I guess you're feeling the same way. If you are feeling like I was, then I think I understand how you must be feeling.'* Saying 'I understand' implies a superior knowledge or being patronising, and that is likely to make the situation worse. Showing you have an insight into how cross or upset someone is helps to defuse it.

■ It's easy to walk away from a row, or from conflict – especially if you are feeling threatened. That is not to say hang around and get a punch on the nose. Leave before that might happen! But if you feel threatened by what someone is saying to you, resist the temptation to put the shutters up and become non-communicative. You won't resolve the situation by freezing it. Try to keep lines of communication open.

■ If you find you are furious with someone, you've become Mr Angry! Or Mrs Enraged! Focus on the issue that has ignited all this ire and find a question to ask. So when a colleague lets you down with a deadline, a workmate leaves the phone ringing for ages or one of the family has left their shoes at the top of the stairs, ready to send you tripping from the top to the bottom, look for the request. *'Dick, could I ask you to get that work onto my desk by tomorrow morning, please?'* Or *'Tracey, would you please pick up the phone and see who it is?'* And *'Can I ask whoever has the size five sandals to come and put them away please?'* Why make a request? Step one, thinking of the right request to make provides a nanosecond for you to put the matches away and forget about lighting the fuse. Second, it stops you turning an issue into a wider conflict.

▨ Become a mirror, or a tape recorder. If someone is sounding off in an aggressive, threatening way, repeat the exact words they have used to upset you. Play them back exactly as they have used them. *'So, Maureen, you're saying...'* (then repeat it back). The chances are, when the person has heard what he or she has said, he or she will see how inappropriate or hurtful it is and calm down. Sometimes you have to repeat the words more than once. This technique keeps the focus on one issue and prevents the conversation from throwing itself off an irredeemable height. In management guru speak, it's called *centring* and keeps the issue in narrow focus.

▨ Accept when you are angry but don't try and shift the responsibility for your emotions to someone else. It's your anger, so you be accountable for it. Try to say *'Peter, I feel very cross when you deliver projects to me late and don't warn me that you are running behind schedule.'* That's much better than *'You make me furious when you're late with stuff!'* Spot the difference? There's no transference of blame, and it leaves Peter only to explain his lateness and not have to deal with your anger as well. Subtle, but it works – really, or your money back!

▨ Become a Libran. Yes, I do understand that not everyone can be born between 23 September and 22 October! It is the sign that is worth the thought: the scales. If you are trying to manage a conflict, picture yourself putting each side of the argument into the scales. Become like a judge, summing up a court case. Be fair to both sides: *'On the one hand I do see that engineering couldn't have delivered the project on time because sales had not given them the customer's drawings. On the other hand, engineering knew the job was needed in eight weeks and should have asked for the information they needed. However, sales could have been more aware of how non-delivery would jeopardise the whole project. I guess everyone carries their share of the blame. What do we need to do to put it right and make sure it doesn't happen again?'*

■ Take your emotions for a workout. Think of controlling your emotions like building muscles and stamina at the gym. Take pride in controlling your temper, in the same way a bodybuilder takes pride in bigger biceps. Get a tight grip on self-control, hold on to your coolness. The more you practise being calm, the better you will get at it. When conflict stares you in the face, say to yourself, this is an opportunity for me to be self-controlled, calm and relaxed. The more you do it, the better you'll be at it. Promise – or your money back!

■ Feeling intumescent? At the point of incandescence? Do nothing. If you know you are about to turn into an Exocet missile, keep off the trigger. Put some time between you, the others and the incident. If someone's stupidity has jeopardised everything you've been working for, concentrate on what has to be done to salvage it. Letting someone know how you feel might make you feel better but won't sort the problem. Putting some time and distance between you and the 'idiot who caused all this grief' will take the intensity out of the emotion, and you'll be better able to establish the truth and get to the bottom of the foul-up.

■ From time to time you'll give yourself permission to be angry. Do it with dignity. No slamming doors, no table-thumping, no throwing things. It frightens people, others will laugh at you and most important of all, everyone will remember the day you smashed the chair into the PC screen. You'll be remembered as the screen-smasher. You'll be perceived as unpredictable, and that is a step away from unreliable. Going to lose your cool? Do it with decorum and chose your words with care. Be remembered for being smart, not a smasher-upper!

24

And, finally, finally...

If all this talk of difficult people is depressing you, think of the people who make you happy, the folks who delight you, the ones who you look forward to seeing and who light up your life. The colleagues who are a pleasure to work with and the associates who are reliable, honest, open and fun.

How to deal with *them*? As the universe, galaxy, world, continent, country, county, town and where you work make more and more use of technology to manage their information and messaging, it is easy to forget one of the greatest motivation tools of all. It is simple and becoming an endangered species. It is being eclipsed by e-mail, messaging, texting and data transmission. The simple and best tools are probably on your desk, right now. They are pen and paper. Never overlook the power of the handwritten note. A thank you card, a note to say well done, can have a huge impact. Use a handwritten note to highlight how well someone has done.

Drop a note to colleagues: *'I've sent a note to Mary to say how well I thought she handled that tricky situation with the Oxford account. Don't you think she did a great job?'*

Write to your boss (why not): *'Thank you for helping me through a difficult time, I really appreciate it.'*

Drop a note to your clients and customers: *'I wanted you to know how much we appreciate the chance to take care of your supply-chain needs. We'll, do our very best to give you great service.'*

...and, really finally:

Thank you for buying this book. I hope it is useful for you!

RL

References

Bramson, R M (1988) *Coping with Difficult People*, Anchor Press/Doubleday, Garden City, NY

Croner's (no date) *CCH Employment Law Manual*, Croner's

Keating, C J (1984) *Dealing with Difficult People*, Paulist Press, Ramsey, NJ

Keyton, J (1999) Analysing interaction patterns in dysfunctional teams, *Small Group Research*, 20(4) (August), pp 491–503

Lewis-Ford, B K (1993) Management techniques: coping with difficult people, *Nursing Management*, 24 (March) (available online from: ABI Inform: www.csuchico.edu: proquest. umi.com)

McRae, B (1998) *Negotiating and Influencing Skills: The art of creating and claiming value*, Sage, Thousand Oaks, CA

Peters, T J and Waterman, R H (1982) *In Search of Excellence*, Harper and Row, New York

Raffenstein, M (2000) Dealing with difficult people on the job, *Current Health*, 2, 26(5) (January), pp 16–22

Rosner, B (2000) Surviving sceptics, dealing with Doubting Thomases at work, *ABC News*, March (available online from: http://www.abcnews.go.com/sections/busines.com)

Webster's (1995) *Webster's II New Riverside Dictionary*, Houghton Mifflin, Springfield, MA

Further reading

Arnot Ogden Medical Centre (no date) Self care: difficult people (available online from: www.aomc.org/Hod2/general/stress-Difficult.html)

Cole, L L (1995) Dealing with difficult people, *Executive Excellence* (January) (available online from: http://proquest.umi.com/)

Executive Edge (1996) How to handle difficult people (available online from: www.smartbiz.com/sps/arts/exe104.html)

Holtje, J *201 Ways to Deal with Difficult People*, McGraw-Hill, USA

Kottler, J A (1994) Working with difficult group members, *Journal for Specialists in Group Work*, **19**(1) (March), pp 3–8

Landolt, S and Hochgraf, L (1997) Dealing with difficult people, *Credit Union Management* (November) (available online from: http://proquest.umi.com/)

Sammy's place (no date) Six types of difficult people at work and how to avoid conflict with each (available online from: http://members.aol.com/spers62774/six.html)

Solomon, N (1990) *Working with Difficult People*, Prentice-Hall, Englewood Cliffs, NJ

Strom-Gottfried, K (1998) Applying a conflict resolution framework to disputes in managed care, *Social Work* (September) (ABI Inform: hostname: EBSCOhost)